HOW TO DO QUALITATIVE INTERVIEWING

Sara Miller McCune founded SAGE Publishing in 1965 to support the dissemination of usable knowledge and educate a global community. SAGE publishes more than 1000 journals and over 800 new books each year, spanning a wide range of subject areas. Our growing selection of library products includes archives, data, case studies and video. SAGE remains majority owned by our founder and after her lifetime will become owned by a charitable trust that secures the company's continued independence.

Los Angeles | London | New Delhi | Singapore | Washington DC | Melbourne

BETHANY
MORGAN BRETT

KATY
WHEELER

HOW TO DO
QUALITATIVE
INTERVIEWING

Los Angeles | London | New Delhi
Singapore | Washington DC | Melbourne

Los Angeles | London | New Delhi
Singapore | Washington DC | Melbourne

SAGE Publications Ltd
1 Oliver's Yard
55 City Road
London EC1Y 1SP

SAGE Publications Inc.
2455 Teller Road
Thousand Oaks, California 91320

SAGE Publications India Pvt Ltd
B 1/I 1 Mohan Cooperative Industrial Area
Mathura Road
New Delhi 110 044

SAGE Publications Asia-Pacific Pte Ltd
3 Church Street
#10-04 Samsung Hub
Singapore 049483

Editor: Michael Ainsley
Senior assistant editor: Charlotte Bush
Production editor: Victoria Nicholas
Marketing manager: Ben Griffin-Sherwood
Cover design: Shaun Mercier
Typeset by: C&M Digitals (P) Ltd, Chennai, India
Printed in the UK

Library of Congress Control Number: 2021932629

British Library Cataloguing in Publication data

A catalogue record for this book is available from the British Library

ISBN 978-1-5264-9734-5
ISBN 978-1-5264-9735-2 (pbk)

At SAGE we take sustainability seriously. Most of our products are printed in the UK using responsibly sourced papers and boards. When we print overseas we ensure sustainable papers are used as measured by the PREPS grading system. We undertake an annual audit to monitor our sustainability.

For Jen

BRIEF CONTENTS

DETAILED CONTENTS

LIST OF TABLES AND FIGURES

List of tables

List of figures

ACKNOWLEDGEMENTS

There are many people without whom this book simply would not have been written.

First, we were both undergraduate and postgraduate students in the Department of Sociology at the University of Essex so we both owe a huge debt of thanks to the incredible training we received from our lecturers over the years.

Second, we would like to thank the University of Essex Summer School who accepted our proposal in 2013 for an introductory course on qualitative interviewing for social science postgraduate students. It was through this experience of compiling a course together that we developed much of the material within this book. The book is equally indebted to our years as undergraduate and postgraduate methods teachers and dissertation supervisors, during which time we have seen first hand the need for this resource.

Third, we would like to thank all our anonymous reviewers for their thorough read of our drafts and for their extremely encouraging and useful feedback, which has helped shape and strengthen this book. And a particularly large THANK YOU goes to our ever-patient editor Michael Ainsley and the team at SAGE for their unwavering support and motivation for us on this project.

Next, we would like to thank our families for their endless support and patience:

Bethany – thank you to all my family, and in particular my loving husband Bryan who always helps to ground me and always believes in me.

Katy – thank you to my husband, Luke, for his love and patience. And to our new son, Arthur, who was just a dream when this book was commissioned. Thanks also to my parents for everything they do to support us.

Finally, we have written this book through some extremely trying times, including serious illness, bereavements, pregnancy and new motherhood, not to mention a global pandemic! But as co-authors, co-instructors on the Essex Summer School course, colleagues and best friends, we have always been there for one another.

PREFACE

How to do Qualitative Interviewing offers an accessible, engaging and practical approach to doing qualitative interviewing. It is organised around a series of practical hints, reflexive tasks, bite-sized pieces of information, and original case study material, designed to engage students and researchers approaching interviewing for the first time. The authors' candid accounts of their research experiences and conversational style bring this resource to life. Unlike other texts on the market, the specific focus here is to offer clear, concise guidance on conducting a qualitative interview, rather than theorising about qualitative research in general or analysing data – discussions of which are often discipline specific.

This is a textbook to be used primarily in undergraduate methods and dissertation teaching. We envisage it as a resource that students can use to learn about qualitative interviewing and then revisit over the course of their fieldwork for the practical tips and guidance. Both authors have extensive experience of teaching on methods and dissertation modules within the social sciences and we co-teach a postgraduate course entitled 'Qualitative Interviewing' at the University of Essex Summer School. We teach students just starting out on their research journey, with the most common methodological choice being qualitative interviewing. However, most methods modules only dedicate one or two hours to teaching this method, and by the time students reach their dissertation module, they have forgotten much of this training. We see this resource as bridging the gap between teaching and entering the field. It is the hand-holding, step-by-step guidance that students need as they navigate the qualitative interviewing process.

How to use this book

As educators and researchers, we feel there is a gap in the market for an accessible, easy to understand, creative and practical guide to conducting qualitative research interviews. We wanted to create a pedagogical resource for both educators and learners, which could be used as a quick point of reference, designed around short, bite-sized, jargon-free sections, written in a candid, fun and engaging style, which draws on our own research experiences.

If you are a student keen to learn how to do qualitative interviewing: The book is designed to be a practical guide and handy resource to support you on your research journey. We have aimed to make it as accessible as possible, with lots of activities for you to undertake from the point of deciding whether interviews are the right tool for your project through to recruiting participants and managing the research encounter. We imagine you using the resource in methods courses when you are formerly trained in research skills, but also at a later stage when you are embarking on your own independent projects and in need of a refresher on key points. The book is tailored to specific moments in the research journey and can be referred to as and when you face obstacles in your practice.

If you are an instructor of research methods: This book is designed to take some of that pressure off university teachers who deliver the principles of qualitative interviewing at level 5, but, when it comes to the practical application of these skills within the dissertation module, find themselves repeating the basics again – with recurrent calls for help on question design, gaining access, approaching the research ethically, and the practicalities of interviewing (e.g. making sure the interviewer has a tape-recorder and has chosen a quiet space in which to conduct the interview). This book can be used as a pedagogical resource, with the student completing the different activities which they then take back to class or supervision, building their results and reflections into their projects, dissertations and theses.

Meet your instructors

Hello, I am Bethany Morgan Brett. I am an academic in psychosocial and psychoanalytic studies, and a child and psychodynamic therapist. I have 18 years of experience of using social research methods, primarily qualitative interviews and psychosocial observations. My first research job was as a research assistant on a project exploring substance misuse in Essex (UK). In the first six months of this job, I had interviewed over 70 people, from people living on the streets, to support workers, to the police. I was really thrown in at the deep end! But this was a really valuable way of developing my interviewing skills and adapting my style for different populations.

My own research has primarily been on the experience of human development, ageing, care and the end of life. My postgraduate/doctoral research explored the experience of ageing during the midlife phase, and I was particularly interested in the connection between death anxiety and the 'midlife crisis'. My current research is on the care and death of older parents in later life.

I have always been interested in the way that people communicate, particularly when they are trying to communicate something emotionally difficult. What is left unsaid and why? Why is something expressed in a particular way and what might that say about the unconscious defence mechanisms at play? I discovered Hollway and Jefferson's (2000) book *Doing Qualitative Research Differently* when I was doing my first masters degree, and it was this approach to interviewing that inspired me to think of interviews in a more psychodynamic way.

Hi, I'm Katy Wheeler and I'm a sociologist with over 15 years' experience of conducting qualitative interviews. My first experiences with interviewing were terrible – I was employed as a research assistant after my undergraduate degree to interview European environmental NGOs. I went into the field with no training in qualitative interviews. With my interview guide in hand, I met with 12 representatives in Brussels and conducted what I now understand to be structured interviews. I did not move from my interview guide and I ploughed through each question in order. It was only once I was formerly trained in qualitative interviews by the wonderful Liz Spencer that I realised how awful these interviews had been. I have since conducted about 150 interviews on subjects varying from Fairtrade consumption to public health interventions, waste management, coffee farming and environmental education. I have experienced qualitative interviewing both as interviewer and participant and have also seen the different way that journalists conduct interviews whilst employed at the Open University, making educational documentaries. I have made lots of mistakes along the way but as this book will show you, it is these mistakes that made me the interviewer I am today. I firmly believe that you only become better at interviewing with practice and careful reflection on each encounter that equips you to improve next time.

Chapter by chapter guide

Each chapter has been written by one of us primarily and we will often refer to the other author when we are writing. In Chapter 1, we introduce the qualitative interview. We discuss why interviews are a popular social science tool and what sorts of data can be gathered using this method. Many students assume they will do interviews in their research projects, but this chapter problematises this assumption. By the end of this chapter, you should know whether qualitative interviewing is right for your research topic/question.

In Chapter 2, we introduce you to different qualitative interviewing styles (including structured, semi-structured, feminist, oral history, life story and free-association narrative interviews), identifying their key features, strengths and weaknesses. In writing this book at the time of the COVID-19 pandemic, we are aware that many researchers are turning to the online space to conduct their interviews, so we include a dedicated section on this mode of interviewing here. You will also find lots of tips and advice about interviewing online throughout the whole book.

Chapter 3 takes you through the key stages of developing an interview guide and interview questions. In our experience, this is a task that students really struggle with so our step-by-step guidance will show you how you can translate your research ideas into well-phrased interview questions. Much of this chapter is organised around frequently asked student questions about interview guides.

In Chapter 4, we help you to identify who your interview participants should be and how you can access them. We guide you through a five-step process to find participants for your qualitative project. The chapter includes useful information about how to design recruitment materials and write contact letters, as well as guidance on working with gatekeepers and providing incentives.

Chapter 5 discusses the key ethical challenges of conducting qualitative interviews, through real-life scenarios and case studies drawn from our own research experiences. We teach you how to gather informed and valid consent from participants. We consider additional elements of the consent process such as mechanisms of withdrawal and anonymisation. We also look at whether written or verbal consent is preferable, and how this choice needs to be matched to the requirements of the participants.

In Chapter 6, we take you through the practicalities of getting ready to go into the interview encounter, including choosing the right location, considering your safety as a researcher, and recording the encounter. We discuss the pros and cons of interviewing in public versus private spaces, and interviewing in online spaces, and what difference this can make to the data collected. We consider recording techniques, such as the use of dictaphones, Zoom, mobile devices, note taking and memory.

In Chapter 7, we focus on key interviewing skills and how to manage the flow of the interview. We discuss the key stages that most interviews pass through and the role of the interviewer at each stage. We stress the importance of using your interview guide flexibly, asking follow-up questions that probe for more depth and detail, the power of silence and the art of active listening. This chapter offers crucial guidance for anyone wishing to create data using the interview method.

In Chapter 8, we ask you to reflect on your own interviewing practice and how your personal biography can affect the data that is collected. We consider the concept of impression management and that how we act in certain encounters can affect the way people think about us – and in turn how this can affect the kind of data that is collected in an interview. We cannot change the impression our participant might have about our age, race, and to a certain extent gender, so it is important to consider how these factors can affect the interview relationship and the data collected. We ask you to think about different combinations of interviewers and interviewees and what difference each might make to the stories that are told.

In Chapter 9, we identify the key practical and ethical challenges of interviewing people in three distinct groups: older adults in residential care, children in school, and elites in the workplace. We explore issues such as the use of physical space and the importance of gatekeepers in accessing these sometimes hard-to-reach populations, and we assess how power differentials within an interview can impact the research data collected.

In Chapter 10, we show you how to transform your audio-recorded interview data into high-quality written transcripts. We consider different transcription styles and how to match the style to your theoretical approach. We evaluate the options on who should do the transcription and the implications of these decisions. Should you transcribe your own data? Pay a professional transcription service? Or use an automated software program? Finally, we demonstrate the importance of clear file naming and keeping your transcripts safe.

Chapter 11 will prepare you for the next stage of analysing and writing up your data. We use this final chapter to highlight the key things you have already done to start analysing your data (in particular, the reflexive journal we encouraged you to begin in Chapter 1), and point you in the direction of sources to help you continue this process. We briefly touch on the key principles of thematic analysis and cover how you can use quotations effectively in your essays and research reports.

All names in case studies, exercises and examples, drawn from our own research experience, have been changed to protect the confidentiality of those involved.

1

INTRODUCTION

Learning objectives

On completing this chapter, you should be able to:

- Understand why interviews have been a popular social science research tool
- Recognise the different sorts of data that qualitative interviews can produce
- Assess whether qualitative interviewing is appropriate for your topic.

Interviews are all around us from the news journalist who interrogates the politician on a podcast, to meeting with your GP to diagnose your ailments, to the nerve-wracking experience of trying to land your dream job. Most people understand what is meant by the term 'interview'. We live in an 'interview society' (Atkinson and Silverman, 1997; Gubrium and Holstein, 2011), where the use of face-to-face interaction to reveal something about people's lives, experiences and attitudes has become commonplace. The social sciences are no exception and the in-depth or qualitative interview – the subject of this short handbook – is the most popular qualitative research tool.

Box 1.1

Stop & Reflect

What comes into your head when you hear the word interview?

There are many images that might have come into your head, but most of them will likely involve two people, with one person doing the questioning

(Continued)

and the other the answering. The interviewer will be interested in what the interviewee has to say and will be listening to their answers to build up a picture of the interviewee and the way they talk about their social world or something they have experienced. Both parties understand that this is the goal of the interview – that the interaction offers a unique insight into the lifeworld of the interviewee.

You may be drawn to interviews for your undergraduate or postgraduate research project as a result of living in the 'interview society'. This book is intended to help prepare you to plan and conduct a project that uses qualitative interviews. One of the downsides of living in an 'interview society' is that many students think they already know how to conduct qualitative interviews. In our experience as both educators and researchers, students who go into the field without training in the art and skill of the qualitative interview end up collecting poor research data. This book will help you to avoid this mistake!

We (Bethany and Katy) have over 30 years of combined experience in conducting qualitative interviews and we have made many of the mistakes we are going to try to help you to avoid. This book has been written as a practical guide to aid you as you start your own independent projects using in-depth interviews. We use examples from our own research to give you insights into how to plan and do qualitative interviews, and we hope you can learn from some of our mistakes and successes along the way.

This chapter offers a brief overview of the research interview and outlines some of the assumptions about data generated in a qualitative interview. It then asks you to consider whether interviews are the right method for your project. Drawing on our experiences of working with many students, we reflect on some of the common difficulties students face when embarking on a qualitative interviewing project. Here we look at the strengths and weaknesses of qualitative interviewing and help define the 'scarier' terms like epistemology and ontology. By the end of this chapter, you will know whether qualitative interviewing is the appropriate tool for you.

Defining the in-depth interview in social research

There are many variations of interviews within our everyday lives, but the term in-depth interview holds a very specific meaning in social research settings (please note that we use the term in-depth and qualitative interview interchangeably in

this book). In Chapter 2, we introduce some of th
while here, in the bulleted list in Box 1.2, we offer a
tures of the in-depth interview.

Box 1.2

Common features of an in-depth interview

- An in-depth interview is an interaction based on dialogue between an interviewer and an interviewee. This is similar to a conversation but an interview is a 'conversation with a purpose' (Webb and Webb, 1932: 130)
- The interviewee has expertise or direct experience of the topic under discussion which the interviewer seeks to uncover
- The questions an interviewer poses should be open-ended and non-leading, in order to encourage the interviewee to share their meanings, stories and experiences in their own words
- The interviewer will usually have several questions, themes or topics they want to cover within the interview, but these will be discussed flexibly to allow for unexpected themes/issues to be explored
- The interviewer should probe for more depth and detail around the topics to make sure they have fully understood what the interviewee has told them
- In-depth interviewers try to create rapport with those they interview and, unlike other types of interview (such as a job or police interview), there is an attempt to minimise the power imbalance between the interviewee and the interviewer. However, this is not always possible as differences of class, gender, age, ethnicity and social status can complicate this goal
- The length of an in-depth interview will vary, depending on the topic under discussion, the talkativeness of the interviewee and the approach to interviewing adopted by the interviewer. But, as a rule of thumb, an in-depth interview will typically last at least 45 minutes to an hour, and it is not uncommon for them to last longer
- Most in-depth interviews involve a single encounter between strangers, but some varieties of in-depth interview rely on multiple interviews
- Ideally, in-depth interviews are conducted face-to-face to maximise the opportunity to build rapport, however, increasingly, they are being conducted using online video-conferencing software like Zoom or Skype
- The knowledge constructed within an in-depth interview is a consequence of the interaction between the interviewer and the interviewee. Both parties are working hard to generate the data and this data is affected by the nature of this encounter.

---

arch interview

rich data about individual experi-
tic use within social research is a
have always made use of informal
ach was not formalised into a dis-
as not embraced as a standard data
Brinkmann, 2018; Brinkmann and
s, 2018; Platt, 2011).

ws in social research was Charles
s. Booth used interviews, alongside
d the social conditions of the pov-
e USA in the 1920s and 1930s, The
techniques when they documented
n they wrote little about their craft.

In the field of psychology, ~~org~~ psychoanalytic theory was based on many hours of therapeutic interviews with patients. His insights were taken up by Ernest Dichter whose book, *The Strategy of Desire* (1960/2012) was based on interviews he conducted in the 1930s with consumers about their motivations for purchasing a car. His work marked the beginnings of the market research interview so common today.

Following the Second World War and the rise of the standardised survey interview, people became more accustomed to offering their opinions and providing information about their lives to strangers which had little direct benefit to them (Gubrium and Holstein, 2011). There was a growing 'democratisation of opinion', whereby individuals were understood to be able to offer useful insights into their experiences and lives. It was not acceptable to only seek the opinions of a chief community commentator or political representative. Ordinary citizens could divulge important and interesting information about their lives which could then be used to better understand public opinion. With a growing interest in qualitative methods evidenced through specialist textbooks and the rise of market and government research bodies, the in-depth interview became a standard tool of social research.

Although interviews have been widely adopted as a legitimate research method, they were initially viewed with much distrust. Many of the objections to interviewing will be familiar to students of the modern interview. For example, WI Thomas, one of the authors of *The Polish Peasant in Europe and America* (1918/1958), reflected on the difficulties of working within different communities and commented that 'the ordinary inhabitant has a singular interest in misleading the outsider and putting a different face on things' (cited in Lee, 2008: 312). Debates about interviewing across difference and the ways the identity of the interviewer influences what data is collected, remain central to current-day discussions about interviews – and are a central feature of this textbook!

The important point to take from this brief history is that research interviewing has not always been the most common way of producing research knowledge. Despite its privileged position today, it is worth taking a moment to stop and reflect on the peculiarity of a complete stranger being willing to share intimate details of their life with a researcher simply because they have been introduced as an interviewer. The expectations and norms of the interview have been constructed over many years, so that many of us are now familiar with the goals and purposes of an interview. These norms affect both how interviews are conducted by the researcher and experienced by the researched.

Box 1.3

Stop & Reflect

What expectations do you have about what it means to be interviewed by a researcher?

You might have thought about expectations around who talks and who listens, who sets the agenda of the interview, how long the interview will last, the types of questions that should be posed, and how the information gathered is likely to be used. This book will help to clarify your role as an interviewer and will encourage you to reflect on the impact these expectations will have on the interview encounter.

Why are in-depth interviews so popular?

The in-depth interview is the most popular qualitative research tool because of the unique access it offers researchers to rich information about individual experiences, memories, stories, feelings and interpretations. This sentiment is nicely captured by Brinkmann and Kvale (2015: 1):

> If you want to know how people understand their world and their lives, why not talk to them? Conversation is a basic mode of human interaction. Human beings talk with each other; they interact, pose questions, and answer questions. Through conversations we get to know other people and learn about their experiences, feelings, attitudes, and the world they live in. In an interview conversation, the researcher asks about, and listens to, what people themselves tell about their lived world. The interviewer listens to

their dreams, fears and hopes; hears their views and opinions in their own words; and learns about their school and work situation and family and social life.

Indeed, we have both used interviews in our own research to great effect. Katy has used interviews to learn how issues like Fairtrade consumption, waste management and environmental education are instituted at the local, national and cross-cultural level, talking to policy makers, private companies, activists and consumers. Bethany, meanwhile, has used narrative interviews to understand how people negotiate the experience of ageing as they enter midlife, and cope with their older relatives moving into care. She has interviewed people who have ageing parents, care home residents, and care home staff. It is hard to imagine another method that could have captured these very diverse issues in such a rich and detailed way. Interviews are an incredibly flexible and versatile method that can be used with a wide range of people from elites/experts in government to vulnerable populations, and for a wide range of topics.

In-depth interviews are popular because they allow the researcher to meet their aims, at the same time as allowing the interviewee to talk about the things that matter to them. Their key strength is the opportunity they offer the researcher to ask questions relevant to the research, and to follow up and probe around the answers the interviewee offers. The flow of the interview means that new aspects of the topic can emerge, and the researcher is able to check they have understood what the participant has told them. This interactive and responsive approach creates useful data that reflects the concerns and priorities of both the researcher and the researched.

For the in-depth interview to reach its full potential, the interviewer needs to be skilled in the art of listening and formulating good follow-up questions. Interviewers need to be truly curious about what their participants tell them, and confident enough to hear where to probe for more depth and detail. Unlike mechanistic methods such as the structured survey questionnaire, which can be carefully crafted, scrutinised and tested before use, the data collection tool in the in-depth interview is you – the researcher/interviewer. Yet the interviewer, like any human being, is fallible. Fortunately, there are many things you can do to prepare yourself to conduct high-quality interviews and we will introduce tools to help you reflect on and analyse what happened within an interview encounter, even if it went badly!

Table 1.1 lists some of the key strengths and weaknesses of in-depth interviews. We will be dealing with each of these points in more detail as we move through the book. You will see that many of the weaknesses can be addressed with careful planning, preparation and practice, though they cannot be completely overcome.

All methods have strengths and weaknesses and the important thing is that you are honest with your audience (examiners, funders, readers) about how you have collected your data and any potential challenges you have faced.

Table 1.1   Strengths and weaknesses of in-depth interviews

Strengths	Weaknesses
• Gives you access to rich data about your participants' experiences, memories and feelings	• Quality of the data depends on the skill and experience of the interviewer
• Is responsive to issues important to each individual participant	• The interview data generated is inextricably linked with the identity and disposition of the interviewer (although some see this as a weakness, we maintain that it is a key feature of qualitative data; it is something to be reflexively engaged with rather than dismissed outright as a weakness)
• Allows researcher to probe for more depth and detail	• Interviewees may present inaccurate information
• Is a flexible and versatile method	• Is time-consuming and potentially costly for researchers to organise, conduct and transcribe
• Is ideal for exploring sensitive issues and for accessing hard-to-reach/'at risk' populations	• Is time-consuming for interviewees which may put some off from participating
• Sample sizes tend to be small and focused	• Smaller samples may carry the risk that key segments of a relevant population are not included
• Non-verbal information, such as body language and intonation or the design of personal space (when conducting interviews in people's homes), can be observed to give a fuller picture of the interviewee	• Can be challenging to analyse and compare interviews because each interview will be different
• Participants often enjoy being interviewed and listened to intently	• Can be difficult to conduct in-depth interviews in cross-cultural settings where the interviewer and the participant do not share the same language

What does it mean to gather data in a qualitative interview?

It is important to open this textbook with some discussion of the nature of knowledge production and the philosophy that underlies the qualitative interview method. You might be wondering why you need to know about philosophy and abstract theory. And in many ways, we agree with you – we have written this book from a practical perspective, with the aim of teaching you how to *do* qualitative interviews. Developing a deep understanding of qualitative methodology is undeniably important but we believe that for a novice researcher, methodological debates often seem removed and can make qualitative research feel inaccessible. So, this is the only chapter where you'll see any real engagement with theoretical assumptions, and this is deliberately a light-touch introduction. Should you want to deepen your knowledge of qualitative research assumptions, we encourage you to read widely in the area (Brinkmann and Kvale, 2015; Denzin and Lincoln, 2018; Flick, 2014; Lincoln et al., 2018). To get you started, we think that there are three key debates you need to be aware of if you plan to use qualitative interviews. These are the ontology and epistemology of qualitative research, knowledge construction within the interview, and the reflexivity of the interviewer. We deal with each in turn.

Box 1.4

Stop & Reflect

Think about what you already know about the definitions of qualitative and quantitative research. What do you recall as being the key differences between the two approaches?

You might have remembered a simple difference – that qualitative research is associated with words, whilst quantitative research uses numbers. (You might remember this by thinking about the L in qualitative referring to Letters, and the N in quantitative referring to Numbers.)

Qualitative research tends to be driven more by the participant, is interested in uncovering meanings through unstructured or semi-structured methods, and is based on small samples to create thick descriptions that are used to build theory (the inductive approach). Quantitative research, on the other hand, is driven by the researcher, is highly structured in its approach, and generates statistical data that is used to test hypotheses and theories (the deductive approach), with sample sizes that are usually large enough to represent wider populations.

Researchers in the qualitative tradition are more interested in understanding phenomena and experiences, whereas researchers in the quantitative arena focus on trying to explain the causes of phenomena. These differences in approach relate to differences in the way researchers understand what exists in the social world and how best they think it can and should be studied. In short, they relate to differences in the ontological and epistemological positions.

The ontology and epistemology of qualitative research

In our experience, students find the terms ontology and epistemology daunting and a little 'scary' when they are learning about the assumptions behind research. Debates relating to the nature of social reality and how we can know about it are challenging and cause confusion, even amongst experienced researchers. But a basic understanding of these positions is important because they shape our methodological choices and will influence what type of interview it will be appropriate to use. We do not offer all the answers here, but in the interest of simplicity we offer the following working definitions of these terms.

Ontology refers to the theory about the nature of social reality, about the relationship between the world 'out there' and our human interpretations of this world. Central ontological questions are whether social reality exists independently of our interpretations and whether there is a common shared reality or multiple context-specific realities. There are three main ontological positions – relativism, realism and critical realism. Relativism accepts that there are multiple constructed realities and no single truth. Conversely, realism assumes that there is a single reality that is knowable through research. Meanwhile, a critical realist position adopts a middle point between these two poles and accepts that a reality exists 'out there' but we can only ever have partial access to it (see Braun and Clarke, 2013). Relativist and critical realist positions are common in qualitative research, whilst realist positions are more common in quantitative research. However, some qualitative evaluation researchers do align their position more with a realist stance to develop accounts of causal processes within complex social situations (Maxwell, 2004; Pawson and Tilley, 1997). Take a moment now to think about where you sit on this continuum, as it will inform how you approach social research.

Epistemology relates to debates about what counts as acceptable knowledge and what it is possible for us to know. Epistemological positions are closely related to ontological positions because what you think about the nature of social reality will inform how you think you can know about this reality. There are two central camps – positivism and constructionism/interpretivism. A positivist position involves using systematic methods to observe and measure a single reality. Following established scientific principles is central to producing objective and value-neutral knowledge that is unbiased by the researcher or research process. Constructionist and interpretivist positions, on the other hand, hold that knowledge is constructed through the process of research, which results in multiple ways of knowing the social world. These knowledges relate to the social, cultural, political and moral contexts which the researcher and the researched are both located within. Knowledge is therefore always subject to interpretation and the researcher (and their biases) is inevitably implicated in the meaning-making and research process.

Although the above suggests a sharp distinction between the ontology and epistemology of qualitative and quantitative approaches, the situation is more complex than that. When it comes to qualitative interviewing, there are different perspectives on how knowledge is generated through this method. It is possible to approach qualitative interviewing from a positivist position, as well as from the more common constructivist/interpretivist position.

Knowledge construction within the qualitative interview

Brinkmann and Kvale (2015) offer two helpful metaphors for thinking about the different perspectives on interview knowledge that map onto the different epistemological positions. On the one hand, there is a view of the interview as a process of knowledge collection, which is likened to a miner digging for treasure:

> In a miner metaphor, knowledge is understood as buried metal, and the interviewer is a miner who unearths the valuable metal. The knowledge is waiting in the subject's interior to be uncovered, uncontaminated by the miner. The interviewer digs nuggets of knowledge out of the subject's experiences, unpolluted by any leading questions. (Brinkmann and Kvale, 2015: 59)

You can probably recognise elements of a positivist approach to social science research in the miner metaphor. It suggests that the interviewer can access a single truth from the head of the interviewee and that this knowledge remains stable both before, during and after the interview encounter.

On the other hand, there is a view of the interview as a process of knowledge construction between the interactions of the interviewee and the interviewer, which is likened to a traveller:

> The interviewer-traveler … walks along with local inhabitants, asking questions and encouraging them to tell their own stories of their lived world. The potentialities of meanings in the original stories are differentiated and unfolded through the traveler's interpretations of the narratives he or she brings back to home audiences. The journey may not only lead to new knowledge; the traveler might change as well. The journey might instigate a process of reflection that leads the traveler to new ways of self-understanding. (Brinkmann and Kvale, 2015: 60)

In this second metaphor, you can probably recognise the constructivist/interpretivist approach to social science research. It offers an account of the interview as an active process of meaning-making between both parties, which has the potential to be transformative.

These two metaphors represent 'contrasting ideal types' which have different rules of the game and assumptions. Concerns have been raised about the traveller approach because if knowledge is constructed in the context of the interview, then what status does this knowledge have beyond the interview? Can participants really give you access to a reality that exists beyond the interaction in which it is generated? Similarly, concerns have been raised about the miner approach because we know that the interviewee is not a 'passive vessel-of-all-answers' whose responses are unaffected by the questioning style or identity of the researcher (Gubrium and Holstein, 2011).

There is certainly tension between the two extreme positions, and most qualitative interviewers find some middle ground between them (Brinkmann and Kvale, 2015; Miller and Glassner, 2016; Rubin and Rubin, 2012; Yeo et al., 2014). We share the position of these researchers. We believe that interviews involve the construction of knowledge within the context of the interaction, but we also see the interview as being meaningful beyond that context. However, in accepting this pragmatic epistemological position, we argue that interviewers must actively reflect on the nature of the interaction within the interview and acknowledge and discuss any potential biases and assumptions that have shaped that interaction. In positivist research, bias is seen as something to be avoided at all costs. But in constructionist approaches, there is an acceptance that it is not possible or desirable to eliminate all biases or assumptions. Instead, 'researchers need to be cautious not to impose their expectations on interviewees and should remain aware of how their expectations affect what they see and hear' (Rubin and Rubin, 2012: 16).

The reflexivity of the interviewer

Reflexivity is a concept we return to throughout this textbook. Some scholars have argued that reflexivity is the defining character of qualitative research in current times (Finlay, 2002). Reflexivity refers to a process of critical reflection on the role that the researcher plays in co-constructing data, in terms of how it has been produced and how it is interpreted. All interviewers come to the interview encounter with their own 'personal baggage' – they have their own values and interests, assumptions and biases, as well as their embodied identity and background (their appearance, gender, age and ethnicity, for example). All these factors will have an influence on interview interaction and how easy or difficult it might be to establish and maintain a rapport with the interviewee.

There are different ways of thinking about and practising reflexivity (Braun and Clarke, 2013; Finlay, 2002; King et al., 2019; Le Gallais, 2008). We like Braun and Clarke's (2013) distinction between 'functional reflexivity' and 'personal reflexivity'. Functional reflexivity involves thinking about how our research tools and process might have influenced the research. In the case of qualitative interviewing, there are different types of qualitative interview styles – from semi-structured to feminist, life-story and narrative (see Chapter 2). The types of stories and data you can gather through these different approaches will differ. For example, a semi-structured interview, where time for discussion is limited to an hour on a series of topics developed by the interviewer, is likely to create quite different data to an open-ended interview where the interviewee is given free rein to talk about what they want for as long as they want.

Personal reflexivity is about making the researcher visible as part of the research process. The interviewer has physical, socio-demographic and psychological attributes that influence the encounter. For example, in Bethany's research on experiences of ageing in midlife, she was a young, White, female researcher interviewing older men and women about a range of experiences relating to getting older. She sometimes found that her participants acted strangely towards her (occasionally defensive, hostile, envious or ashamed) and this led her to think carefully about how her identity might have influenced her interview data and interpretations. You can read more about this in Chapter 8.

It is not enough to just state your identity; there needs to be a real engagement with its significance for the research undertaken. This is easier said than done, but one way to start this process is to keep a research diary/journal so that you can record your feelings and thoughts on the interviews you conduct. Do not rely on your memory as you will forget. The journal can also help demonstrate the validity or 'trustworthiness' of your approach (Lincoln and Guba, 1986; Noble and Smith, 2015). We will keep reminding you about the research journal as we think it is very important.

Activity 1.1

Starting your reflexive journal

Getting into the habit of keeping a reflexive journal to record the process and experiences related to your interviewing project is really important. Make a start today by deciding how you will keep your journal – will you have a notebook to take notes by hand or will you create a file on your computer? You could explore some online private journalling apps like Penzu (https://penzu.com) and Journal-ate (https://myjournalate.com), where you can record writing and include images and videos. The advantage of the online journal is that you can complete it whilst you are on the go, but you may want to back up your journal in some way just in case the website closes unexpectedly. Once you have decided how you will keep your journal, make your first entry by writing about the following things:

a. Why are you interested in your topic? What has led you to have this interest? What assumptions do you already have about your topic?
b. Who are you? How might your identity impact your project? For example, if you are a man who wants to interview young women about their food practices, how might this influence the data you can collect? You can't step outside of your body to become someone different, so think in advance about possible ways your identity might influence your data and how you could use your identity to your advantage.

Deciding whether interviews are right for your project

Now you have a clearer idea of what an in-depth interview is, what sort of data you can collect through interviews and how it came to be such a popular research method in the social sciences, it is time for you to decide whether qualitative interviewing is the right method for your project. Many students come to us assuming their projects will involve qualitative interviews – often because they want to avoid statistics. But this is not the best criteria on which to base your decision. Instead, you should base your decision on whether your research question is best answered using qualitative interviews and, as described above, whether your position on the nature of knowledge construction aligns with the philosophy of qualitative interviewing.

Defining your research question is a challenging and exciting part of any research project. (We do not provide detailed guidance on developing a research question here, but if you are struggling to come up with and refine your research question, we recommend the following sources: Aurini et al., 2016; Mason, 2002; O'Leary, 2017; Punch, 2014; Silverman, 2017). What we focus on here is recognising the types of research questions that can be answered using qualitative interviews.

Types of research questions/topics for qualitative interviews

The qualitative interview is a flexible and versatile method so there are many occasions where interviews are appropriate. Research questions that begin with 'how' and 'what' tend to be most suited to qualitative research, whereas those focusing on 'why' and 'how much' are more suited to a quantitative approach. Research questions that focus in on how people experience the social world and attach meanings to those experiences are likely to be well suited to qualitative interviews. Qualitative interviews allow you to place the information gathered into the context of an individual's unique biographical history. This means you can make connections and comparisons between different interviewees' experiences, so that nuanced and complex accounts of the social world are developed.

Qualitative interviews are good for exploring research questions that deal with sensitive topics (like sexual encounters, health problems or experiences of discrimination). For example, Bethany's project asked how people make the decision to place older parents into care and she found this sensitive issue was best addressed through interviews where she could build a rapport with her interviewees and give full attention to each unique story.

Interviews are often used when other sources of information are unavailable about a topic. For example, when researching how an environmental education programme came into being in Scotland, Katy found that although there were many documents about the policy decisions made, there was little information about how the different organisations came together and worked to achieve those policy goals. Qualitative interviews were the most effective way of gathering this information.

Interviews can also be used within mixed-method research designs, either alongside other qualitative approaches or within a sequential design where interviews are used to help develop and interpret survey questions and responses (Creswell, 2013). Researchers trying to understand an under-researched area or how a topic is understood by diverse populations might use a series of qualitative interviews (and focus groups) to help develop closed-ended questions for large-scale surveys. Conversely, findings from surveys might be examined in greater detail through qualitative interviews, either with a small sample of those who completed the survey or a new sample (see, for example, Silva et al., 2009).

Box 1.5 provides a useful summary to help you decide whether your research question is suited to a project that uses qualitative interviews.

Box 1.5

How to decide whether your project should use qualitative interviews

- You are interested in how something is/has been experienced or done
- You want to understand an individual in the context of their unique biographical history or experiences
- You want to explore the perceptions and understandings of someone with a 'personal stake' in or direct experience of your research question/topic

- You need access to the ways people talk about an issue
- You need specialised and detailed information about a project, a service or an organisation that cannot be accessed in any other way (via documents, for example)
- You want to explore a sensitive issue (like placing older relatives into care, or sexual experiences) and you need to ensure confidentiality and build rapport.

When qualitative interviews might not be appropriate

Students often make the mistake of assuming that when their project asks a 'how'-type question, interviews are the best choice of method. In fact, there are many other qualitative methods that could be more suited to your project. If you are interested in the way people in general understand a particular phenomenon and you do not need your participants to have a personal experience of this topic (for example, understandings and meanings associated with a media or political figure/issue), you might find that focus groups are a better tool than interviews. From experience, we know how difficult it is to ask people to talk at length and in detail about something they have little interest in or direct experience of; whereas, within a focus group, people can interact with others and discuss issues with more freedom, from different perspectives. Focus groups offer great insights into collective understandings, with group interactions providing rich access to diverse ways of talking about topics and how meanings are constructed (see Bloor et al., 2001; Braun and Clarke, 2013; Stewart et al., 2011).

You might be interested in how people organise more mundane everyday practices in the home or workplace (like cooking, shopping or dealing with residents in a care home environment). Whilst people may certainly speak at length about what they do within a qualitative interview, you might find observation or ethnographic methods are better suited to capturing how people operate and act out of habit. Using observation, you might gain richer insights into the context in which taken-for-granted habits and understandings are performed (such as how people deal with food waste or make purchasing decisions) than asking people to rationalise these practices verbally. Observation allows the researcher to pay attention to visual cues and body language which participants themselves might not be aware of. Often, researchers use observation alongside interviews to give them access both to what people say about their practices and what they do in practice (Hammersley and Atkinson, 1995; Lofland et al., 2006).

Qualitative researchers are interested in social processes rather than in easily defined variables and identifying cause-and-effect relationships (Silverman, 2017). However, many students come to us with research questions that define such relationships up front – these are more suited to a quantitative approach. For example, a student came to Katy whose research question was 'How do age and gender influence the acceptability of sustainable fashion options?' The student wanted to use qualitative interviews, but the research question was not appropriate for this method. The student had assumed age and gender were the key factors influencing the uptake of sustainable fashion options, and to discover if this was the case, she would have needed access to data from a broad cross-section of the population. The research question was changed to make it more suitable for a qualitative interview approach – she asked 'How do millennial consumers understand and engage with sustainable fashion?' When developing research questions for qualitative interview projects, be sure to avoid building in assumptions about the nature of the issue under study.

Table 1.2 provides a quick reference summary of the sorts of research problem or question that might be better served by a method other than qualitative interviews.

Table 1.2 When your project might be better suited to another research method

Your research aims	What other methods you could use
You want to uncover general attitudes to a particular social phenomenon	Focus groups; questionnaires
You want to understand what people do in the course of their everyday work, leisure or home life	Participant observation; digital ethnography; visual methods
You need an accurate account of how an event or a service was/is publicly represented	Document or media analysis
You want to identify trends within a large population, possibly to make predictions about future behaviours	Questionnaires; survey data
You want to assess the cause of an outcome and you can identify which variables are likely to be responsible before you start your study	Experimental design; survey data

To give an example of the ways research questions influence the choice of method and the decision of whether qualitative interviews are right for a project, we use an example from Katy's research (Case study 1.1).

Case study 1.1

Real research in action

Katy conducted her PhD research into Fairtrade consumption and support within the Fairtrade town of Chelmsford, UK (Wheeler, 2012). The main and sub-research questions for the project were as follows:

Main question: How do people understand and engage with the Fairtrade movement?

1. What does it mean to be a Fairtrade supporter living within a Fairtrade town?
2. How do those without an expressed commitment to Fairtrade understand the Fairtrade choice?
3. How do people evaluate the effectiveness of Fairtrade consumption? Does gender, social class and age influence how people evaluate its effectiveness?

Stop & reflect

Can you guess which research question in the project was the most suited to qualitative interviewing?

If you selected sub-question (1), you are right. The first sub-question is best answered using qualitative interviews because Katy was keen to find out how committed Fairtrade supporters came to be involved in the local Fairtrade movement and how they organised their support of this cause within their everyday lives. It was important to place their individual stories in the context of their other experiences and commitments, so qualitative interviews were ideal to answer this research question.

The second sub-question was less suited to qualitative interviews because it is hard for people to give rich and detailed insights into something they have little experience of or 'personal stake' in (Braun and Clarke, 2013: 81). To answer this research question, qualitative methods were still appropriate, but Katy chose to use focus groups as the research tool.

The final question was a little more complex and called for a mixed-method approach. The first part could be tackled through both qualitative interviews and focus groups. The question is about understanding how people evaluate Fairtrade consumption and so it was relevant to ask those who deliberately shop for Fairtrade as well as those without a commitment to the movement, for their opinions of this action. Asking this question qualitatively allowed Katy to explore diverse understandings of what effectiveness might mean amongst individuals with different personal histories of campaigning. The second part of this sub-question

(Continued)

involved searching for general trends within the larger population and was there-fore unsuited to a qualitative approach. Notice that Katy was able to identify at the outset the variables likely to influence people's evaluations. This is usually a clue that a quantitative approach is needed (Silverman, 2017). The aim of this question was to correlate socio-demographic data with opinion data to find a relationship between them, so Katy used survey data.

In a final comment on research questions in qualitative interviewing projects, do bear in mind that it is common for research questions to shift in focus as you con-duct your project. Unlike quantitative projects where it is usual to begin with a hypothesis that needs to be tested throughout the course of the research, qualitative projects have research questions that evolve in the research process. You should be led by your participants and you may find that what you thought was the crucial question is not central to the stories you are hearing. Rubin and Rubin (2012) describe this as a 'responsive' model of research design where you adapt your approach as you learn from earlier interviews and develop your ideas.

Activity 1.2

Is interviewing right for your project?

Write down your research question and assess whether it is suitable for a qualita-tive interviewing project, using the information provided in Box 1.5 and Table 1.2. If you discover your research question is not suitable for qualitative interviewing, what will you do? We recommend you either re-write your question or consider an approach other than qualitative interviewing. If you chose to re-write, remember that qualitative interviewing projects ask 'how' and 'what' questions, are focused on understanding processes or experiences and do not define variables of interest at the outset.

Classroom-based alternative: Look at the following short descriptions of research projects that propose using qualitative interviews. Discuss whether you think these projects' aims can be met using in-depth interviews, using the informa-tion provided in Box 1.5 and Table 1.2. What other methods might the student use? How might the topics be adapted to make qualitative interviewing more appropri-ate? If you think interviews are appropriate, what do you think would be the key strengths and weaknesses of approaching this topic using interviews (use Table 1.1 to help you)?

a. Mark wants to explore the experiences of young Black men who have been stopped and searched by the police in London. He thinks there might be different experiences in two different parts of London, and he wants to see if this is the case.
b. Amanda wants to look at the practice of vegan parenting. She is interested in how families negotiate the attitudes of others towards this choice, as well as how factors like age, gender and class affect this practice.
c. Beatrice is interested in how employees feel about annual leave policies and what changes, if any, they would like to see to their own company's policy.

Top tip summary

- Do not assume that just because you live in an 'interview society' and understand what an interview comprises, you can conduct an interview without some training in the craft.
- Use this book for practical training in interview skills, such as how to listen attentively, how to ask good questions and how to probe for more depth and detail.
- Think carefully about your position on what is knowable about the social world through research, because this will inform your approach to qualitative interviewing.
- If you have a research topic that asks a how-type question and is interested in an individual's experience of an issue/situation, a qualitative interview is probably the right tool for you.
- Start a reflexive research journal today to record your thoughts, assumptions and experiences related to your research project.

2

DESIGN YOUR STYLE

----Learning objectives----

On completing this chapter, you should be able to:

- Identify different qualitative interviewing styles
- Recognise the advantages and disadvantages of each qualitative interviewing approach
- Select an appropriate interview method to address your research question.

Qualitative interviews are used to investigate how people understand and experience the social world. In an interview, the participant is given the freedom to express an opinion, share their feelings or tell their story. The aim of a qualitative interview is to gather interpretations, understandings and recollections. It is about trying to find out how something happened, what a person thinks about a certain topic, or why they responded in a particular way to an event. It is less about getting quantifiable answers to questions of 'how much?', 'how many?' or 'how long?'

We like Rubin and Rubin's (2012) characterisation of the qualitative interview as 'responsive interviewing', which suggests that it is important to adapt your approach according to both the topic under discussion and the type of participant you are interviewing:

> Responsive interviewing ... emphasises flexibility of design and expects the interviewer to change questions in response to what he or she is

learning. Responsive interviewing accepts and adjusts to the personalities of both conversational partners. (Rubin and Rubin, 2012: 7)

In this chapter, you will learn about some of the different styles of qualitative interview. We invite you to think about what kind of data you want to collect and to consider which style of interviewing suits your project. Are you looking to capture a participant's life story? Do you want to record first-hand accounts of a particular historical event? Are you looking to collect data on sensitive or emotional issues? Are you interested in how your own emotions play a role in the interviewing process? Are you looking for short, succinct answers to set questions on a particular topic?

Interviewing styles can range from highly structured, where the researcher uses a set of questions and will not deviate from these, to a more open-ended approach where the participant is able to speak freely without the control of the interviewer. Below, we briefly outline some of the different qualitative interviewing styles, which will help you to design the right style for your project. At the end of this chapter, you will find a table of the different interviewing styles, a summary of what is involved with each approach, and each style's key strengths and weaknesses.

Structured interviews

In a structured interview, the interviewer asks a set of standardised questions from a written interview schedule. In this style of interviewing, the questions are fixed and specific, with little scope for moving away from the schedule. The researcher might have predetermined categories and expect answers which either confirm or disconfirm a hypothesis. This approach is useful when a researcher needs to make direct comparisons between answers from different respondents. It creates data which is consistent and replicable by another researcher. It is a focused approach in which important and relevant information can be gathered quickly and succinctly. However, this approach does not allow for an interviewee's story to emerge or for the researcher to follow up on any leads. Although the data collected might be qualitative, this approach is often used in quantitative approaches such as forming part of a survey.

Semi-structured interviews

Most of the qualitative interview types discussed in the rest of this chapter start from a variant of the semi-structured interview. Semi-structured interviews are a versatile style of interview and can be used to gather different types of information. They can be more or less structured, depending on the interviewee and the topic to be explored. They are the form of qualitative interview that most interviewing text-books, including this one, develop guidance for (Brinkmann and Kvale, 2015; King et al., 2019; Morris, 2018; Rubin and Rubin, 2012; Yeo et al., 2014).

What semi-structured interviews have in common with one another is the use of some pre-formed questions within an interview guide which will be used with all participants. But crucially, the interviewer in this style of interview is allowed (and expected) to explore emergent themes, rather than simply focusing on concepts and ideas defined prior to the interview. The researcher will have some overarching ideas about what they would like to find out from their participant, and they will usually use an interview schedule to guide the direction of the discussion. However, they also have the freedom to rephrase a question, skip a question, formulate new questions, follow up on emerging leads, and probe for more detail from a respondent. The interviewer's role, when conducting standard semi-structured interviews, is to be engaging and encouraging but generally with limited reciprocity or personal disclosure about their own experiences (in contrast to feminist interview approaches).

Case study 2.1

Using semi-structured interviews for a project on waste management

Katy used semi-structured interviews for a project exploring recycling practices and waste management cross-nationally (in the UK and Sweden), as well as within households in the UK (Wheeler and Glucksmann, 2015). The project looked at how recycling systems were organised in the two countries and how consumer recycling habits influence these systems. The data was gathered from 30 expert interviews with public and private waste-management organisations and from 30 household interviews. Semi-structured interviews offered the flexibility to ask all participants several common questions and to tailor and adapt the questions for different participants. Three different interview guides were developed – for experts in Sweden, for experts in the UK and for households in the UK. Common questions included how easy it was for the consumer to recycle, what motivates people to recycle, and what households know about recycling. There was the opportunity to compare and contrast the answers from householders about the things they struggled to recycle, and the information they received, with the data gathered from experts who were designing recycling systems and communication systems for these households. But there was also the opportunity to explore the unique insights from each group of participants – for example, the history of different waste-management organisations and their working relationship with others in the national system, as well as the household dynamics that surround the domestic division of recycling chores.

Feminist interviews

Historically, social scientific research methods have marginalised, inadequately represented, and even excluded, women's experiences. Where the qualitative interview has sometimes been a site for hierarchical, exploitative power relations (Oakley, 1981), a feminist approach to interviewing promotes a reflexive and reciprocal approach to the research relationship (Letherby, 2003; Luff, 1999; Ryan-Flood and Gill, 2010).

Ann Oakley, who pioneered this approach, proposed that this form of interview should include self-disclosure and potentially longer-lasting relationships (even friendships) with your interviewees. In this style of interview, the interviewer focuses on building rapport with their participant, through a mutual sharing of experience, the creation of trust and the co-construction of data. The premise is that a closer relationship with interviewees can produce a more valid and meaningful account of an individual's (particularly women's) experience.

Life story interviews

The life story technique allows for a detailed study of complex relationships of experiences across time, and usually covers the life from birth (or even pre-birth) until the present moment. This type of interview is primarily respondent-led, allowing the interviewee to organise and arrange the stories of their life. However, life stories are naturally very messy. If you have ever tried to write your own autobiography, you will realise that it is extremely difficult to form a focused and coherent narrative, as there are many overlapping streams of events. For example, if you want to tell the stories of your primary school years, it would be very difficult to stay focused on this thread of events without going into detail about your home life too. An interviewer can help guide the interviewee through the different stands of their life, following themes, threads and points of interest.

Life story researchers may be interested in narrative construction, noting where the emphasis of someone's story lies (Atkinson, 1998; Holstein and Gubrium, 2000). Does the participant focus on one particular aspect of their life, as opposed to another? Why does it feature in such prominence, and what might this say about how the participant feels about that life experience?

Life story interviews offer valuable data about specific social, cultural and historical issues, so, for example, a life story interview with someone from the 'Millennium generation' would help situate those experiences within a wider structure around what it means to grow up in that particular period of time. Through the lens of an individual's life story, a researcher may be able to create a connection between personal lives and wider public events.

In a life story interview, the interviewee is encouraged to tell the story of their life as completely as possible. Typically, the interviewer would guide the interviewee through topics such as childhood, schooling, family, early relationships, leisure, hobbies and mealtimes, work history, social life, later family life, marriage, children, grandchildren, friendships, and future dreams.

Oral history interviews

Oral history interviews explore the biographical accounts of those who are key sources of history, tradition and culture, and eyewitnesses to historical events. Oral history interviews have similarities to life story interviews in that they gather personal narratives about an individual's life, but they differ from life story interviews in so far as they are primarily a historical project with a focus on a particular moment in time, and they do not necessarily take the narrative up to the present moment. *The Edwardians* (Thompson, 1992), *Pioneers of Social Research* (Thompson, 2019) and Mike Roper's (2017, 2020) research into the children of disabled soldiers after the Great War, are all examples of this approach in action.

Oral histories typically aim to record and preserve memories of an older generation's first-hand account of an historical event that can be passed on through generations. They provide the opportunity to study history through first-hand accounts of those people who have actually experienced it; in particular, it gives a voice to those who may have been marginalised in society. Through the stories and memories recounted in an oral history, the past comes to life. We are able to learn about ways of life in times gone by, from family traditions to occupations and skills, celebrations, customs and everyday life. These are all powerful expressions of community life, of family life, and of the values and beliefs people held at that point in time.

Oral history interviews often involve the use of visual materials. You might ask your participant to show you old family photographs or other documentary materials such as scrapbooks, old letters, family trees, favourite recipes, heirlooms or other mementos to stimulate further memories.

Free association narrative interviews

Hollway and Jefferson (2000, 2013) outlined a new way of conducting interviews in their influential book *Doing Qualitative Research Differently*. Their approach originated from the research they conducted in their study 'Gender Difference, Anxiety and the

Fear of Crime', in which they found that a traditional semi-structured approach did not work when asking difficult or anxiety-provoking questions.

They developed a free association narrative interview (FANI) approach, which begins with the assumption that a participant is unconsciously defensive when they are asked to discuss sensitive and difficult issues. The technique used to work with these defences is to conduct two interviews with each interviewee. To begin, they use a free association technique in a life story or biographical interviewing method, keeping the questioning style as open as possible, and allowing the interviewee's ideas, views and story to emerge as much as possible in their own words. This free association technique follows the direction of the interviewee's 'ordering and phrasing' of their story (Hollway and Jefferson, 2000: 53). It also allows the interviewer to look critically at any inconsistencies and contradictions, which can then be checked in the second interview through a series of narrative questions based on the first interview. The second interview is the opportunity to ask some more structured questions to make some comparisons between interviewees. It involves asking 'tailor-made' questions based on issues which seemed to cause the conflicts in the narrative. The interviewing process is then followed by a detailed analysis of the experience as a whole – including the relationship between the interviewee and the interviewer, the emotions involved, examining the words in the transcript and a careful consideration of the narrative construction (see Chapter 8 for more detail on this method).

Case study 2.2

Free association narrative interview method in action

Bethany used the FANI method in her 2011 research 'Negotiating Midlife: The Subjective Experience of Ageing'. Taking the lead from Hollway and Jefferson (2000), she conducted two interviews with each interviewee. She originally aimed for the interviews to be one week apart but, due to practical and geographical constraints, this was not always possible and the gap between them was sometimes up to a couple of months. This method of double interviewing her participants was valuable as it enabled her to explore some of the psychodynamics of the first interview and to take this into consideration in the second interview. She was able to follow up on leads, hunches and ideas which arose in the first interview. The first interview was more open-ended than the second. Although Bethany took inspiration from Hollway and Jefferson's method of interviewing, she did not follow it rigidly. She found that a free association method requires a certain amount of courage and it is too easy to revert to the security of the interview guide and its predefined questions. In the initial stages of interviewing, she felt a constant worry and danger that, without this safety net, the conversation would dry up and she would not know how to develop a certain lead (this is an indicator of her own defensive anxiety). Using a guide gives the interviewer a degree of control over the interview, control over the interviewee and even control over themselves to ask the right questions in the right way. For Bethany, it took a few attempts with her own interviewees to relinquish some of this control, and, although she asked some questions, she tried as far as possible in her later interviews to allow the interviewees' narratives to develop according to their own line of thinking. These latter interviews were far richer than previous ones in terms of stories and emotional content.

Activity 2.1

What's your style?

Now you have learnt about different types of interview, take a moment to match your research objectives to one of the types of interviews covered in this chapter.

What do you think you will need to conduct an interview using this approach? What might be some of the advantages and disadvantages of using this chosen approach? You can use the information in Table 2.1 to help you.

Table 2.1   Different styles of qualitative interview and when to use them

Type of interview	Type of interview data created	When to use	When not to use
Structured	Shorter, succinct answers Focused on a set topic	If you want to compare responses across interviews When detailed answers are not required When replicability is required When short on time	When you want to explore feelings or listen to stories When discussing sensitive issues, as this can feel intimidating and impersonal for the interviewee
Semi-structured	Responses to questions about a topic, but also some expression which deviates from the set questions via prompts and probes	When you want to gather responses to or opinions on a topic When you want to make comparisons between responses across interviews	When you want to understand unconscious processes, deeper feelings and emotions When you are interviewing on highly sensitive topics

(Continued)

27

Table 2.1 (Continued)

Type of interview	Type of interview data created	When to use	When not to use
Feminist	Reciprocal and co-constructed data	When you want to represent and validate women's experiences	When you want to gather value-free, unbiased, non-reflexive data
Life story	Stories which are focused on specific moments in the life course, taking the story from birth to present moment	When you want to gather rich descriptions of an individual's life and relationships When you want to see how personal lives fit within a wider social context	When you are short on time When you are only interested in one particular social issue When you want to gather opinions on a set topic
Oral history	First-hand accounts, stories, feelings and memories about a particular period in time	When you want to understand an individual's or a community's values, beliefs and experiences of everyday life as a snapshot in time When you want to preserve the voices of an older generation When you want to hear the experiences of marginalised voices	When you are short on time When you want assurances about the reliability of your interviewee's story
Free association narrative interview	Conscious narrative accompanied by an analysis of the unconscious processes	When you want to understand what it is your participant finds difficult to talk about When conducting research on sensitive topics	When you are short on time When you want to be able to compare responses across interviews When replicability is required

Online interviews

Before we finish this chapter, we wanted to take a moment to think about remote interviewing. As we write this book, we are amidst the COVID-19 global pandemic and many researchers are having to turn to the virtual, online space to conduct their research. The examples in this book are drawn from face-to-face encounters, but we think it is helpful to consider some of the advantages and disadvantages of conducting interviews online. Conducting interviews via an online platform means that we are interacting with our participants in a new and slightly different way. Some researchers chose to conduct research online before the pandemic and there are parallels between online interviews and other forms of remote interviewing, like telephone interviewing (Deakin and Wakefield, 2014; King et al., 2019; Weller, 2017).

Online interviews can be conducted synchronously (held in real time) or asynchronously (in non-real time). Synchronous interviews might be held via a video-conferencing online platform such as Microsoft Teams, Zoom, Google Hangouts, Skype or Whatsapp messenger. Synchronous interviews often have a similar format to face-to-face interviews, with the participant responding verbally or textually to each question as you ask them in real time. Asynchronous online interviews might take place over a period of time, with respondents writing their responses via email, chat functions or discussion groups.

In Table 2.2 and Box 2.1, we focus our attention on the most used method for online interviews – synchronous video conferencing.

Table 2.2 Advantages and disadvantages of synchronous online interviews

Advantages	Disadvantages
Can flexibly fit in with busy or complicated schedules	The lack of co-present, face-to-face contact can make it feel impersonal
	Might be more difficult to build rapport – though you may be able to do some of this work via email exchanges prior to the interview
If an interviewee's home is chaotic, conducting an interview online can release some of the pressure to tidy up or present themselves in a particular way	Body language is harder to read, or even absent
Might suit participants who are socially awkward and would feel uncomfortable (or even might not agree to participate) in a face-to-face encounter	Connectivity can be problematic due to a variety of factors such as location, phone data plans, internet provider, weather, access to electricity, etc.
It is physically safer, in terms of meeting strangers and infection transmission, than being in someone else's presence	Social inequalities can impact on the ability to access technology such as laptops, mobile phones or tablets. This has implications for sampling as you might only be able to contact those in positions of technological privilege
Some households are scrutinised by social care/social work professionals and your participant might feel judged by having you in their home. An online or telephone interview can help avoid what they might see as professional intrusion	It can be difficult to work with silence as it can be mistaken for a connectivity issue. Non-verbal cues are much harder to read online so silences can be especially awkward

(Continued)

Table 2.2 (Continued)

Advantages	Disadvantages
There is lower financial cost and reduced environmental impact as it avoids travelling to interviews	Privacy can be difficult to achieve for some participants. It might be difficult for a participant to talk about a sensitive topic with others around
Some video-conferencing software will automatically generate a transcript of the interview	The automatic transcription will need to be carefully checked for errors, so it may not save as much time as might be imagined

Box 2.1

Top 10 tips for video-conferencing synchronous interviews

1. Begin by sending a calendar invitation for the interview to your participants with a link to the platform you are using or a direct invitation to the online meeting
2. Do not assume your participant is familiar with the platform; give them plenty of notice of the interview, the format it will take and time to install any necessary apps or programs
3. Will you have an expectation for the camera to be on? If switched off, some of the personal interaction and social cues might be lost
4. Check your camera environment. Make sure there isn't anything you would not want your participant to see lying around. Green screens, virtual or blurring backgrounds can be used to hide some of your surroundings. Remind your participants that they can do this too
5. Try to position your camera so that you have good lighting. Avoid having any windows behind you. Position the web camera face-on where possible
6. Check the microphone and audio quality in advance
7. Join 5 minutes early if possible, to deal with any problems, and offer your participant another form of communication (your email address or phone number) in case they have trouble joining the meeting
8. If you are recording the interview, remind your participants of this and gain their consent to record
9. Remind participants to be mindful of who is in their real-life space. Ask them to:
    - find a quiet and private space if possible
    - think about how the topic discussed might be received by the people who can overhear it – if it is a topic which is sensitive or controversial to

discuss in the presence of other people, consider using headphones and typing responses via the chat function

- not leave their camera on and unattended as other people they live with may accidentally appear on screen.

10. Be mindful of time – some online meeting platforms are time limited unless you upgrade your subscription. You may get cut off!

Top tip summary

- Interview styles can range from highly structured to an open-ended approach. Choose an approach which matches the type of data you would like to create.
- Consider the strengths and weaknesses of each interview style before deciding which is right for your project.

3

PLAN YOUR INTERVIEW GUIDE

Learning objectives

On completing this chapter, you should be able to:

- Translate your research ideas into interview questions
- Design and test out an interview guide
- Recognise and write a well-phrased interview question.

So, you've decided a qualitative interview is the right tool to answer your research question and you've thought about different approaches to interviewing. Now comes an important stage that many novice researchers underestimate – the process of translating your research ideas into appropriate qualitative interview questions. This is a surprisingly difficult and time-consuming task and one many students struggle with. It is also a topic not given much attention in introductory textbooks, with more focus usually devoted to managing the interview encounter.

In this chapter, we take you through a step-by-step process, by the end of which you should have developed a draft interview guide, which has been piloted and is ready for final modifications. The chapter is broken down into four key sections, with an activity attached to each section. The sections are: recognising your assumptions; moving from your research question to an interview guide; recognising good and poorly worded questions; and piloting your guide. The activities are designed to bring you along with us, so that if you follow the steps laid out in the chapter, you should end up with a draft interview guide by the end.

Recognising your assumptions

Cast your mind back to Chapter 1 and the reflexive journal you began (Activity 1.1). In your first entry, you were asked to reflect on your research topic, including why you are interested in this topic, what has led you to this interest and what assumptions you already have about your topic. This journal entry is the starting point for developing your interview questions, so if, for some reason, you haven't already made an entry, start now with these questions. Box 3.1 contains Katy's reflections on her interest in Fairtrade and her assumptions about Fairtrade consumers.

Box 3.1

Katy's first journal entry

I became interested in Fairtrade initially after a discussion with my Dad about Fairtrade coffee. He told me that Fairtrade was not always fair to farmers and that I should be less trusting of the Fairtrade movement in general. I also remember sitting in an AGM of the SCAE (Speciality Coffee Association of Europe) and hearing coffee roasters talking about the problems of labelling part of the market as fair and the rest of the market as unfair. There is no monopoly on fairness. This has got me thinking more about my own assumptions that Fairtrade is fair, and I wonder what other consumers think about this label. This is the start of my research question, but I think I also need to be aware that I am now assuming that consumers are being misled about Fairtrade which might not be the case. I am just a casual consumer and my perspective has been influenced by my dad who has his own reasons for challenging this movement. People who are committed to this label will think differently and I need to explore that. I also have an assumption that social class or income is likely to play a role in supporting Fairtrade as a consumer – do people feel guilty and buy to ease their conscience?

Your research interests will probably connect to experiences and conversations you have had and attitudes you hold. They will shape how you move forward in your project, but you must be careful not to let already-held assumptions influence how you will study the phenomenon you are interested in. In Box 3.1, you can see that

Katy held several assumptions as she started her project – Fairtrade is unfair, consumers are being misled, social class will influence consumer behaviour. It was important that she recognised these assumptions at the outset so they did not determine how she proceeded with her research, and that she took care to design an approach that would not just confirm these assumptions.

Interviewers play a very active role in generating data with their interviewees, so they need to be mindful of how their attitudes can influence how they ask questions and how they react to answers (Rubin and Rubin, 2012). Do you hold stereotypes or strong feelings about your potential interviewees, for example? If so, how will you make sure that these preconceptions do not cloud the research process? For instance, if you were to admire a group of individuals or think that a programme they are running is worthwhile, this could prevent you from asking questions about something problematic they have done: 'Rather than pretend that you have no biases, it makes sense to examine how your preconceptions might slant the research and then work to formulate questions to offset your biases' (Rubin and Rubin, 2012: 72).

Activity 3.1

Reflecting on your research question

Have a look at your first journal entry and think carefully about how you will work with the assumptions you already have about your research topic. Make another short entry now about who your potential interviewees are. What do you think they will tell you about your research question? What will they not say? How do you feel about interviewing these people? How do you think your interviewees will respond to you? You will use these reflections as you develop your guide.

Moving from your research question to an interview guide

'A research question is not the same as an interview question': Bethany and I probably say this to every student who comes to see us who is at the stage of developing their interview guide. Given the amount of time it can take to develop a feasible research question, it is not surprising that students sometimes think that once they've worked this out, they are ready to start interviewing. But there is a lot of conceptual and practical work to be done to turn your research question into a list of potential questions to ask within an interview.

Most practitioners advocate spending time developing a guide or protocol of questions – this is sometimes called a 'topic or discussion guide' (Arthur et al., 2014), an 'interview guide' (Braun and Clarke, 2013; Brinkmann and Kvale, 2015) or a 'conversational guide' (Rubin and Rubin, 2012). We use the term 'interview guide' in this textbook. The key thing to remember about your interview guide is that it is a flexible document which has been designed as a memory aid and springboard for discussion. It is not a carefully worded set of questions to be ploughed through in order, regardless of what your participant says.

We have organised this section in the style of frequently asked questions, focusing on the common things students ask us (and we tend to repeat) in dissertation supervisions.

Should I have a guide?

Given that the strength of qualitative interviews is their flexibility and the fact that they are responsive to what your participants say, you might be wondering if you need to spend lots of time developing a list of questions at all. Perhaps you could just turn up to the interview with a few broad questions and then let the interview unfold, following up on your interviewee's answers to these broad questions and developing new questions as you go along. Indeed, as we discussed in Chapter 2, interview guides are mainly used in semi-structured interviews rather than unstructured interviews. In our experience, the majority of students choose to undertake semi-structured interviews, so we would recommend that you do spend time and energy thinking about what you want to ask your participants, how you will ask them and in what order you might do this. Even if you decide not to take the guide with you to the interview, the time you have spent thinking about what to ask and how to follow up will leave you freer to concentrate on what your participant is saying, rather than worrying what to ask next.

How do I know what to ask?

Working out questions that will provide rich data about your research question takes time, but it can be broken down into a series of manageable stages (see Figure 3.1). As already indicated, the first stage involves having a clear research question which is suitable for exploring using qualitative interviews (see Chapter 1 if you are unclear on this).

The second stage requires you to do some independent research around your research question to help you start thinking about what information you will need to answer the question, and how you might approach this. Brinkmann and Kvale (2015) refer to this as the 'thematizing' stage of the interview process because it involves clarifying the purpose of the study and becoming familiar with existing knowledge

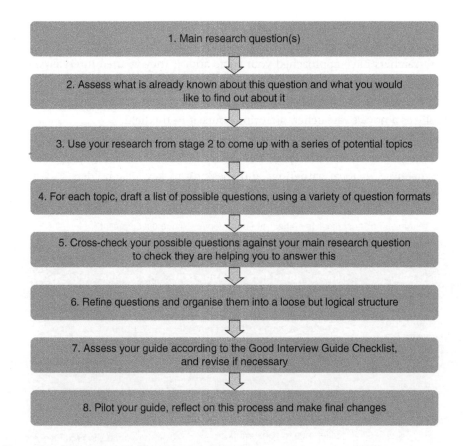

1. Main research question(s)

2. Assess what is already known about this question and what you would like to find out about it

3. Use your research from stage 2 to come up with a series of potential topics

4. For each topic, draft a list of possible questions, using a variety of question formats

5. Cross-check your possible questions against your main research question to check they are helping you to answer this

6. Refine questions and organise them into a loose but logical structure

7. Assess your guide according to the Good Interview Guide Checklist, and revise if necessary

8. Pilot your guide, reflect on this process and make final changes

Figure 3.1 Key stages in the development of an interview guide

about the topic under investigation. There are three main ways to conduct this second stage – (a) asking yourself why this topic is of interest and what things you want to find out, (b) looking at existing academic and other literature about your question and how to approach it, and (c) spending time with people who are similar to your potential interviewees to find out how they talk about the issue.

You should have already started (a) by completing the first activity in this chapter. Look back at this now and think about what sort of interview topics might be appropriate from your own ideas and experiences of your research issue. What assumptions do you have about what it is important to know? What questions would you want to be asked if you were to be interviewed on this topic?

To get started with (b), we recommend you read widely around your research topic. This will inevitably include published academic papers, chapters and monographs. But you should also include other sorts of documents, like newspaper and online blog/thinkpiece articles, newsletters and leaflets that are relevant to your topic area. You should not only be reading about your substantive topic, but also about the style of qualitative interview you will adopt. Different approaches to interviewing call for more or less structured interview guides (see Chapter 2). Look at how other researchers have approached your topic and, if they've used interviews, what style did they adopt? You may even be able to find interview guides that others have written. We believe reading literature is an important part of the research process and, especially as a novice researcher, orienting yourself in the field.

For (c), doing some initial pilot fieldwork is suggested. By this we mean spending some time in the areas where your potential interviewees hang out, or attending public meetings or local gatherings and speaking to key stakeholders so you can

Table 3.1 Moving from stage 1 to stage 3 of your interview guide development

Stage 1: Main research question(s)	Stage 2: Assess what is already known about this question and what you would like to discover	Stage 3: Use your research from stage 2 to come up with a series of potential topics
How do people understand and engage with the Fairtrade movement in the UK?	*Personal reflections:* Whether consumers think Fairtrade (FT) is fair and how they make that judgement; What are people buying as FT and why – or do they even know? How do people learn about FT? What does it mean to live/be involved in a FT town? Who are the FT consumers? Is there a gender/age/social class difference to consumption? *Findings from the literature:* Attitude/behaviour gap (Szmigin et al., 2009) Ethical distinction and social class display (Varul, 2009) Type of consumer who buys FT will often be interested in other ethical labels/practices too (Clarke et al., 2007a, 2007b); shopping is the new politics (Micheletti, 2010); ideas about how to ask interviewees: to link to engagement in other activities, like in Clarke et al. (2007b) *Out and about in a FT town:* Mostly older consumers buying at the stall; linked FT to Christian and charity aims; seem to be a small network of people who know about town status and the rest of the population has little awareness – also discussed in town meetings; no advertising about FT town in supermarkets and local shops	• Shopping practices • Knowledge about Fairtrade • Living in and supporting a Fairtrade town • Identity of Fairtrade consumer • Political/ethical dimensions to Fairtrade consumption

hear how they talk about your research issue and what they see as important. This can be useful for learning about local language – in terms of slang and everyday ways of talking, as well as common acronyms and taken-for-granted ways of referring to something – and for getting familiar with daily routines that your interviewees might be following.

On completing all three steps of stage two, you should draft a list of potential interview topics for the third stage of the design process. Group similar topics together and sort your ideas so that each topic offers a distinct area for exploration in the interview. See how Katy did this for her project on Fairtrade in Table 3.1.

Activity 3.2

Coming up with interview topics

Using the method outlined above, develop your list of potential interview topics. You might decide to lay this out in the same way that Katy has in Table 3.1, or you may prefer to use a more visual format, such as a spider diagram or flow chart.

What sorts of question should be on my guide?

The sorts of question that should make up a qualitative interview depend on the sorts of information you are trying to elicit. Patton (2002) suggests that there are six types of question you can ask to elicit different sorts of information. Table 3.2 summarises these different types of question and offers a few examples of each. It is important to think carefully about what sorts of information you want from your participants and how you can phrase questions to elicit this information. We are not suggesting you need to include all types of question on your guide, but do think about a variety of question types to help you to get at the information you need.

Table 3.2 The six key types of interview question (Patton, 2002: 348–51)

Type of question	Brief description	Examples
Experience and behaviour	Asks what a person does or has done, focusing on actions the interviewer could have observed if present to observe	• How do you organise your food shopping? • Can you talk me through the items you throw away in a typical day? • What was your experience of dealing with the care staff in your mother's care home?

(Continued)

39

Table 3.2 (Continued)

Type of question	Brief description	Examples
Sensory	Asks about sensory aspects of experience – what people say, hear, touch, taste and smell. This is a subset of experience/ behaviour questions but focuses on sensory elements	• What did you say to the local councillor about Fairtrade? • What do you do to manage the smell of food waste in your home? • What do you see when you walk into the care home?
Opinion/Value	Asks about a person's opinions, judgements and values about an issue to find out what they think	• What role, if any, do you think the UK government should play in alleviating global poverty? • What do you think about recycling in this town? • What is your opinion on euthanasia clinics?
Feeling	Asks about a person's emotional response to their experiences. The interviewer is looking for 'adjective responses': anxious, happy, afraid, etc.	• What does it mean to you to live in a Fairtrade town? • When watching the environmental video of the turtle with the straw in its nostril, what feelings did this provoke in you? • How do you feel about your parent going into a care home?
Knowledge	Asks what information a person knows about a policy, situation or process	• What steps must be taken to become a Fairtrade town? • What policies are in place to meet the Landfill 2020 targets? • What sorts of things can the volunteer care workers do?
Background/ Demographic	Asks about a person's identity and personal characteristics – such as age, occupation, marital status. This information is useful for locating your respondent in relation to others, though you might find it easier to collect some of this using a short questionnaire before/after the interview	• Tell me about yourself • What do you do for a living? • How would you describe your ethnicity?

How many questions do I need?

This is a question we are repeatedly asked and unfortunately the answer really is, it depends! It will vary according to how long your interview lasts, what sort of participant you have (either talkative or reticent), what approach to qualitative

interviewing you are adopting (fewer questions would ...
cial interview than in a semi-structured one), and how m...
elicit from your participant about the different topics in ...
would suggest that in an hour-long interview, you are unli...
cover more than five broad topics in depth and you may need o...
main questions per topic. However, we usually recommend that n...
viewers prepare more questions than they think they might need bec...
will be less used to thinking up follow-up questions in-situ. But, as w...
guides, these questions should be used flexibly and only asked if appropriat...
the context of the interview.

How should I structure my guide?

To structure your guide, you need to think about (i) the core elements of an interview, (ii) the flow of the interview and, (iii) how to lay out your guide. An interview is made up of four key elements – the introductory or opening question, main questions, follow-up questions (sometimes called probes and prompts), and closing questions/remarks. Table 3.3 provides a summary of each of these elements and offers examples of each. You might be wondering whether you need to specify all your follow-up questions on the guide as many of these will be formulated in the moment of the interview in response to what your participant says. We would recommend thinking about potential follow-up questions (mostly prompts) in this planning stage so that you are well prepared for the interview, but be ready to ignore, adapt or re-word these follow-ups depending on what your participant says.

Table 3.3 Core elements of an interview

Core element	Description	Examples
Opening questions	The opening questions should be easy for your participant to answer, giving them the chance to feel secure or even proud of something they have achieved. The purpose of the opening questions is to make your participant feel comfortable and to help build initial rapport. Some researchers like to use the opening questions to gather basic demographic details	• How did you come to be involved with the Fairtrade Town group? • How did you first hear about the care home volunteer network? • Tell me about yourself

(Continued)

GUIDE

be needed in a psychoso-
uch detail you want to
your interview. We
ely to be able to
ly one or two
ovice inter-
use they
ith all
e in

	Examples
your opics es of ue with icipant d show or show ppens d	• Can you tell me the story of how Chelmsford came to be a Fairtrade town? • Can you walk me through a typical day in the care home? • How would you recycle (a selection of items)? *Followed by*: What do you think about recycling in this town?
at ....ound by earlier responses when describing what they do. It is also a good idea to place sensitive or difficult questions in the middle or later part of the interview when the interviewee is feeling more comfortable about being interviewed (for more on sensitive interviewing, see Chapter 8)	
Follow-up questions	Follow-up questions explore interviewees' answers in more depth, asking for clarification and elaboration of key concepts, understanding or events. There are two main types of follow-up question: probes and prompts (we explore these in greater depth in Chapter 7) **Probes** are 'questions, comments, or gestures used by the interviewer to help manage the conversation' (Rubin and Rubin, 2012: 118) **Prompts** are issues explicitly raised by the researcher 'rather than issues raised by the interviewee' (Yeo et al., 2014: 196) Prompts are more likely to be on your guide than probes	• Can you say a bit more about that? • Can you give me an example? • What makes you say that? • What do you mean by 'X'? • In what way was it difficult? • Mmm, uh-huh • Nodding, smiling • What about 'X'? • Some people we've interviewed have said that 'Y' is an issue – have you experienced this?
Closing questions/ remarks	The closing questions should give participants the opportunity to say or ask anything that has not been covered by the main questions. Sometimes a question that looks forward can be a good way to close an interview. Closing questions can also be a good opportunity for the interviewer to check that they have understood what the participant has told them	• What are the next steps for the Fairtrade Town group? • Is there anything that you think we should have covered but haven't yet? • I think I understood that you feel 'X' about the community volunteer scheme because of 'Y'. Is that right?

As you can see from Table 3.3, there is an implicit ordering to the different elements of the interview, with an introduction, a main body and a conclusion. You should follow a logical order in your questioning within the main body, for example asking about how a situation started before asking how the participant sees the situation developing in the future. However, the main body of the interview can take different formats depending on the nature of your topic and what you want to find out. Rubin and Rubin (2012) talk about four different types of interview flow which they relate to different objectives and stages of a project (see Table 3.4). When developing your guide, think carefully about which type of interview pattern would work best to help you reach your objectives.

Table 3.4 Different types of interview flow (Rubin and Rubin, 2012: 123–5)

Interview flow	Description
Opening the floodgates	This mode is most common at the beginning of a study when the researcher knows little about the topic, but the interviewee is very knowledgeable. This interview flows around one to two broad main questions, which the interviewee talks about at length, and the interviewer uses probes to find out more
Main branches of a tree	This structure involves dividing the research problem into roughly equal parts, with a main question for each part (a branch). The interviewer gives similar levels of attention to each branch, using probes and prompts to explore each one in detail. Care should be taken that each main question follows logically from the previous one. This interview flow is all about gaining breadth of insight
River and channel	This interview flow is about exploring an idea, concept or issue in great depth to the exclusion of other issues. Like following one channel in a river, the interviewer focuses in on one key theme and develops follow-up questions around that theme. This pattern of interview might occur when your interviewees have different levels of knowledge/experiences and you want to concentrate on the specific expertise of each interviewee
Picking up the twigs	This format is used when conducting a follow-up interview. Often, follow-up interviews are organised in either 'main branches of a tree' or 'river and channel' mode, however you might find, at the end of a big project, that there are several different, unrelated topics that need to be covered – so they are like twigs that need to be picked up

A final aspect of structuring your guide is laying out the content physically. How you choose to lay out your guide will depend on personal preference. Some researchers like to write out all their main and follow-up questions in full, whilst others write brief notes in a bulleted list. The danger in writing questions out in full is that you might be tempted to read them verbatim rather than adapt each question for each interview, though you may feel you need that extra security in your first few interviews. Whatever method you opt for, make sure that key questions/ points on your guide are visible at a quick glance – using tools like bold, italics and colour. Ideally, you should go into your interview with your guide memorised as you should not really break eye contact with your participant to find the next question, so a visually accessible guide is key.

Should I keep my guide the same throughout the whole project?

Unlike in quantitative research where each participant must be asked the same questions in the same order, qualitative interview questions should be flexible and tailored to each interviewee. Your interview guide is a working document to be changed as you move through your project. Be aware that ethics committees might ask for an indicative interview guide before you commence your research, but there is always a big difference between this guide and how questions are asked in practice (Barbour, 2014). You may find that some questions do not work or that new questions emerge following discussions with your participants. You may find that you need more than one guide per project for different sorts of interviewee, following the river and channel flow. In a project Katy conducted on environmental education, she developed different guides for the different organisations based on the expertise and experience of each interviewee. When looked at together, these interviews provided rich data about the topic, but each interviewee was able to offer a different perspective depending on whether they worked for a government, NGO or private organisation.

Activity 3.3

Drafting your interview guide

Look at the list of topics you developed in Activity 3.2 and use the guidance above to help you to draft an interview guide. You will be working on stages 4 to 6 of the interview guide development, such as drafting, cross-checking and refining your questions into a loose structure (see Figure 3.1). Think carefully about what sorts of questions you need to ask and how you imagine the interview will flow.

Box 3.2 offers an example of an interview guide for Katy's Fairtrade project which was conducted with committed Fairtrade supporters, involved in the Fairtrade Town network. Notice how questions are organised under each of the main topics. One of the main topics identified in stage 4 ('Identity of the Fairtrade consumer') was removed as a key sub-heading but is covered by the other questions in the guide. This guide is provided as one example of an interview guide and follows the 'main branches of a tree' flow, using a selection of scripted questions and bulleted prompts. In fact, this is not the guide that Katy used for her PhD as there were many mistakes in the original one, which will be discussed in the next section.

Box 3.2

Katy's example interview guide for committed Fairtrade supporters

(Note: Interviewees were asked to have a recent food shopping receipt ready for the interview.)

　　Introduce self and project, explain we will start with shopping practices before moving on to questions about Fairtrade and their interest in this.

* Warm up

Please tell me a bit **about yourself**

　　Probe around household composition, work, hobbies

* Shopping practices

Describe your food **shopping routines**

　　Probe: Where? How often? Who does it?

(Using their recent food shopping receipt as a prop) Talk me through **what you tend to buy**

　　*Probe: Why? How **typical** was this shop? Changes over time?*

If applicable – how far are **other members** of your household involved in choosing the products you buy?

　　Prompt: What do you look for when shopping for your children?

What products on your list are Fairtrade products?

　　Prompt: Did they try to buy these as Fairtrade products? How easy to find them?

Are there any items here that you could have bought as Fairtrade, but chose not to? If so, what was the reason?

(If there are any other ethical consumption choices on the list, explore these as above)

(Continued)

- Knowledge about Fairtrade

How did you become aware of/learn about Fairtrade?

Probe: How they got involved, key influences

What was it about Fairtrade that made you want to support it?

What do you know about the benefits of Fairtrade to farmers in developing countries?

Prompt: Ever seen the impact by visiting a developing country or met a producer?

Are you aware of any criticisms? If so, how do you respond to them?

- Political/ethical dimensions to Fairtrade consumption

Why is it important to **you** personally to support Fairtrade?

Probe: Around faith, activism, other types of campaigning/ethical consumer activities

How does your **family** respond to your support of Fairtrade? And your friends?

Probe: Any conflict or difference of opinion?

What is your opinion of the idea of 'Trade not aid'?

Some people have said that **shopping choices are the new ballot box** – what do you think of this?

*Prompt: **How effective** do you think individual shopping choices are in alleviating poverty in developing countries?*

- Living in and supporting a Fairtrade town

Can you tell me the story of how Chelmsford became a Fairtrade town?

Probes: Key steps to become a Fairtrade town? How did they persuade key actors to support Fairtrade? Any activities they are particularly proud of?

How did you get involved in the Fairtrade Town group?

How would you describe the make-up of the Fairtrade Town group?

Probe: What groups/people are not represented?

What does being part of a Fairtrade town mean to you?

What actions is the group involved in currently?

What are the next steps for the Fairtrade Town group?

- Closing

Is there anything that you think we should have covered but haven't yet?

Recognising good and poorly worded questions

Box 3.3

Stop & Reflect

What makes a good qualitative interview question?

You might have thought about questions that are non-leading, are truly open, ask about one thing at a time, are free from jargon/abstract concepts, are clear, and follow up on what the interviewee has told you. In general, good qualitative interview questions seek to elicit views from the participant's perspective and do so using straightforward, open language.

Now you have your draft interview guide, you need to evaluate whether your questions are well worded and appropriate.

The most common mistake that novice researchers make when developing their interview guide is that they create questions that are very leading and assumption-laden. Look back to the first activity you undertook in this chapter and remind yourself of the key assumptions you have about your research question and interviewees. These assumptions might represent important hunches, but care must be taken that you do not design questions that simply reinforce these assumptions. For instance, Katy highlighted that one of her assumptions about Fairtrade consumers was that they are likely to be well-off, with disposable income. An assumption-laden, and therefore poor, question, seeking to confirm this hunch, would be:

Do you think you need lots of money to buy Fairtrade?

This question does not invite the participant to offer their own perspective and instead assumes a predetermined direction that is influenced by the researcher's assumptions. This question is also a closed question which could be answered with a simple 'yes' or 'no', and is therefore unlikely to generate rich, qualitative data. A better way of getting at this idea would be to ask:

What sort of person do you think buys Fairtrade? Or Who buys Fairtrade?

These re-written versions make no assumptions about the characteristics of the Fairtrade consumer and instead ask the participant to give their view.

Recognising good and poorly worded questions is an important part of developing your interview guide. Table 3.5 outlines some of the key characteristics of well-worded questions and offers examples of when things go wrong. What generally happens when these principles are ignored is that the interviewee is led to think that there is a desirable response, or they misunderstand what is being asked of them. The questions discussed are real examples from our early research practice and we include our reflections on what happened when we asked these questions – you will see that we have often violated more than one principle when we asked the poor question in the second column. In the third column, we offer an alternative way of wording the questions that would have yielded better qualitative data.

Table 3.5 Characteristics of well-worded questions

Good interview questions should be ...	Example of when this principle is ignored	What happened and how could we have fixed it?
Open-ended	Was your childhood happy?	If you ask a question like this, it might elicit a 'yes', 'no' or very short answer which will not tell you very much about a participant's experience of childhood. Qualitative interview questions should open up a discussion rather than invite a one-word response. The question is also quite leading because it assumes the interviewee's childhood should be defined in terms of happiness
		If you mistakenly do ask a closed question like this, you can open up the 'yes' reply through using a probe such as 'What makes you say this?' But a better question would be
		Can you tell me about your childhood?
Assumption free	Do you think that religion plays any role in your involvement in the Fairtrade movement?	When Katy asked this question, the response she received was 'I'm not particularly religious, so I'm not a great person to ask!' The problem was that her pre-existing assumptions about who the Fairtrade supporters are pre-defined the wording of the question. This is also a closed question and does not invite a full response from the participant
		A better way of getting at this is to ask the question in a more open way without assumption:
		What makes you support the Fairtrade movement?
Non-leading	Is buying Fairtrade a way of making a difference?	Leading questions are those that are phrased in a way to invite a respondent towards a particular response. They are very similar to assumption-laden questions, but there is a subtle difference. This question led the interviewee towards a specific proposition that was difficult to disagree with – in fact, everyone asked this question agreed with it! It is also a closed question
		An alternative would be:
		Why do you buy Fairtrade?

Good interview questions should be ...	Example of when this principle is ignored	What happened and how could we have fixed it?
Clear and simple	Do you get ideas about what are good manners and what are bad manners from western influences?	In Bethany's first ever research project as an undergraduate, she explored different cultural understandings of manners. But she struggled to develop a clear and simple question about this. She hadn't thought that the concept of 'manners' itself was likely to be understood quite differently in different cultures. When she asked this question, her Indian respondent did not understand what 'manners' meant as a concept. She found herself having to explain her own definition of 'manners' as she understood it, which led her participant to simply just agree with her. The problem was that with such a multi-faceted concept, one question was not likely to do justice to it. A series of clear and simple questions was needed, depending on different dimensions of the concept, such as: *What do you understand by the term 'manners'?* *What is considered respectful behaviour in your culture?* *How do people expect to be treated by others in your country? Can you give an example?* *What happens if they are not treated in this way?* *Do you see any differences between your country and the UK?*
Jargon-free	What are the main lessons that policymakers and SMOs/MACs in your country/region can learn from experiences in other countries in the environmental/ GMO field?	This was from one of the first interviews that Katy ever conducted. She did not develop this question but asked it (at least the first time she did an interview)! It relies on acronyms that were developed by the project team and the participant needed help to understand what she was asking. It is important to use language your participants understand. This also helps to make the question clear and simple A revised version is: *What are the main lessons that environmental policymakers and civil society organisations in your country/region can learn from the experience of other countries?*
Single	What do you like or dislike about being your age at the moment?	Questions should always ask a single thing at a time because if the question is double-barrelled, interviewees tend to answer the last part of the question rather than the first. This meant that Bethany initially received lots of comments about what people disliked about their age. She later asked the questions separately, e.g. *What do you like most about your age now?* *What do you dislike most about your age at the moment?*

The suggestions in Table 3.5 are general principles and there will be certain situations where it is necessary to violate them. For example, an evaluation study might have questions that are more assumption-laden because it will be expected that problems and successes in achieving programme goals will be part of the interview. Similarly, interviews with experts or professionals will often contain jargon because this is the language these interviewees are used to working with (and it will likely involve some learning by the interviewer to be fluent in this language).

The good interview guide checklist in Box 3.4 outlines the key features of well-prepared interview guides. You can use this to check your interview guide and to assess the questions you have developed.

Box 3.4

Good interview guide checklist

- Your interview questions address your research question
- The opening question is easy for the participant to answer
- Sensitive questions are placed towards the middle or end of the guide
- Experience/behaviour questions are asked before opinion/value questions
- There is a logical flow between each main question or section of the interview
- The interview closes with an opportunity for the participant to add their final thoughts/reflections
- There are not too many/ too few questions/topics covered in view of how long you will have for the interview (this will be a judgement call but ask yourself whether you can achieve the depth and breadth you need through these questions)
- The guide is easy to read at a quick glance
- Questions are open
- Questions are clear and simple
- Questions use appropriate language (free from jargon; language interviewees would use)
- Questions ask a single thing at a time
- Questions are not assumption-laden (they encourage the participant to give their perspective)
- I would feel comfortable in answering these questions.

Piloting your guide

We cannot stress enough the importance of testing out or 'piloting' your guide before you start organising the main interviews in your study. You do not want to spend a

Activity 3.4

How good is your guide?

Assess your interview guide according to the good interview guide checklist in Box 3.4. Have you made any mistakes? How might you correct them?

Optional classroom-based alternative: Swap your interview guide with a class member and assess each other's interview guides using the checklist. Feed back your comments to your colleague. It is sometimes hard to notice our own mistakes so getting a colleague to review your guide is a useful exercise.

lot of time and effort recruiting your interviewees only to find the guide does not flow how you thought it would, the questions are misunderstood or you are not getting the data you had hoped for. You could recruit just one participant who fits your sampling frame (see Chapter 4) or someone similar to your prospective participants – or even just a colleague, friend or family member. Use this encounter to practise your interview questions. To make the pilot effective, you need to carefully reflect on what went well and less well, and adjust your guide as a result of this reflection. So, it would help if you recorded the interview so you can listen to it back. You may decide you want to conduct more than one pilot interview so that you can evaluate how well any adjustments work in another interview. To help you with this process, Box 3.5 lists some questions to help guide your reflection on pilot interviews.

You should also use the pilot as an opportunity to reflect on your performance as an interviewer, assessing any strengths or weaknesses in your practice. Turn to the guidance in Chapter 7 to help with this.

Box 3.5

Questions to ask yourself after piloting your interview guide

- Did the interview flow as I expected?
- Did I use the guide flexibly?
- Did I cover all the questions?
- Were the main questions understood by the participant?
- What questions worked well? Why?
- What questions worked less well? How can I adapt them?
- Did I follow up effectively on what the participant said?
- Would I ask the same follow-ups again? Are there additional follow-ups that I could have asked? If so, should these be added to the guide?

Activity 3.5

Pilot and reflect

Pilot your interview guide and reflect on this process using the questions in Box 3.5 to help you. Make any changes to your guide that you think are appropriate.

Top tip summary

- Do not underestimate how long it takes to develop an interview guide, and remember that a well-developed and thought-through guide will save you time in the long run as you are more likely to gather useful interview data from it.
- Start your interview guide by making a reflexive journal entry which records your initial assumptions about your research question and your potential participants. Your guide should not seek to merely reinforce these assumptions.
- You can search for inspiration for your main interview topics from your own experience, the research and popular literature, and by hanging around your research site or talking to key stakeholders.
- Your interview guide should include an appropriate range of different question types (see Table 3.2) and these should be cross-checked against your main interview topics and your main research question.
- The number of interview questions you need will depend on your interviewee and their expertise in your topic, as well as the depth and breadth of content you want the interview to cover.
- Use the good interview guide checklist (Box 3.4) to assess your interview guide for common mistakes and to avoid poorly worded questions.
- Pilot your interview guide and reflect on this process, before starting to recruit and organise interviews with your main interview sample.

FIND PARTICIPANTS

A successful interview study needs interviewees – this chapter will help you to identify and recruit your participants. Qualitative sampling is something that students report difficulties with, and it is common to see student projects that rely on a handful of easily accessible friends rather than carefully selected interviewees. This chapter takes you through a step-by-step guide for a robust recruitment process to help you collect rich and useful data that offers unique insights into the topic under study. Friendship networks can certainly have a place in this. Careful thought into how you will identify potential participants and encourage them to take part in your research, must happen early in the research process because this information will be required for ethical review boards. The chapter begins by introducing our step-by-step guidance, before focusing in on each step in more detail. Throughout, we highlight and answer frequently asked questions in relation to each step.

Step-by-step guide to finding interview participants

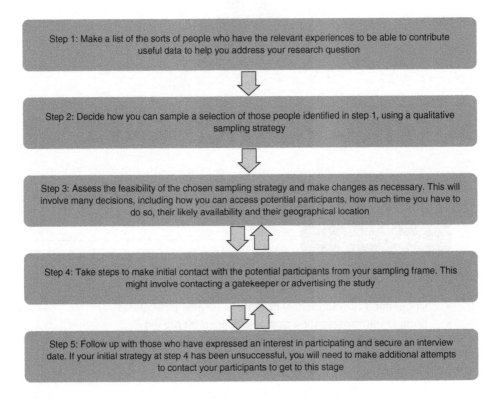

Step 1: Make a list of the sorts of people who have the relevant experiences to be able to contribute useful data to help you address your research question

Step 2: Decide how you can sample a selection of those people identified in step 1, using a qualitative sampling strategy

Step 3: Assess the feasibility of the chosen sampling strategy and make changes as necessary. This will involve many decisions, including how you can access potential participants, how much time you have to do so, their likely availability and their geographical location

Step 4: Take steps to make initial contact with the potential participants from your sampling frame. This might involve contacting a gatekeeper or advertising the study

Step 5: Follow up with those who have expressed an interest in participating and secure an interview date. If your initial strategy at step 4 has been unsuccessful, you will need to make additional attempts to contact your participants to get to this stage

Figure 4.1   Step-by-step process for recruiting interviewees

Figure 4.1 summarises the key steps needed to identify and recruit participants for your interview study. As you will learn throughout this chapter, some steps will be more important or take more time than others, depending on the nature of your research topic and the characteristics of your potential participants. Nearly all interview studies will involve each of these steps.

Step 1: Identifying your population

This first step involves making a list of which groups of people are most likely to offer useful and relevant data to help you answer your research question. Interviewees are selected because they have particular experiences or hold knowledge that will offer rich data. This step might sound obvious, but it is not necessarily straightforward and does require careful thought. If you are researching something relatively few people are likely to have experienced (for example, a rare medical condition) or which requires direct involvement in a small programme or specific policy, your list of potential participants is going to be limited. This compares markedly to a research problem for which all people will have some relevant experience, such as Bethany's project on the experience of ageing. In either case, whether the potential list is limited or much broader, there are many choices and considerations to take into account.

In a project about obesity interventions, Katy was conducting a process evaluation of a community gardening scheme. The aim of this evaluation was to assess how far the programme activities had been implemented as intended, so the pool of potential participants was relatively small. Within this study, it was important to gather the views of both those responsible for delivering the programme, and those who were using the gardening scheme. Choices needed to be made about whether all users of the gardening scheme should be included in the population or whether it would be better to speak only with those who had been involved from the beginning. Similarly, there was a member of staff who was involved in the setting up of the programme but who had since moved on, and a decision had to be made about whether this person should be a potential participant or whether only current staff would be the population.

Bethany's project involved interviewing people who were in the period of midlife, about their experiences of getting older. The available population for this research problem was very large. Some of the choices she needed to make to identify her population included thinking carefully about how to define the period of midlife as this means different things to different people, about whether she was interested in those who had just entered this phase or had been in this phase for some time, and about whether she was interested in how women or men or both sexes experience the ageing process. For each of these decisions, the size and scope of her study population changed. These choices will always come back to the key aims for your study and what data you need to gather. Even at this step, it is worth thinking about the feasibility of accessing this population and whether you have existing networks to aid in the recruitment process.

Can't I just interview my friends?

When identifying their population, students can fall back on the 'easy' option of assuming an existing friendship network will do. This is often because research questions are influenced by the student's own experiences and their friendship group will have likely also had these experiences. It can feel less daunting to approach friends rather than strangers when recruiting interviewees.

Friendship networks can and often do play an important role in identifying potential participants, but you must exercise some caution and ask yourself whether it is this ease of access that is driving your approach rather than the suitability of your friends to offer relevant data.

Although you might think it would be easier to interview friends than strangers, it can be quite difficult to conduct interviews with someone you know well because of the existing knowledge you have about them. In qualitative interviews, you need to ask detailed follow-up questions and probe for more depth, and this can be harder to do if you have an existing relationship with the person. You may already know the context of what they are telling you so you fail to ask the obvious questions that would provide the best data. You also need to think about the ethics of interviewing friends – does the existing friendship make them feel obliged to take part, for example? What if they reveal something that changes your relationship with them? Will they hold information back because they don't want to affect the friendship? On the plus side, developing rapport in the interview may be easier with a friend than a stranger.

The answer to this question is not a simple one, but decisions about your study population must always come back to who is most likely to be able to offer relevant and rich data for your project. Only use friends if they can meet these criteria.

Step 2: Moving from the study population to a sample

Your study population are all the potential people who could be interviewed for your project. Your sample is the selection of people you interview from this larger population. The criteria you use to make this selection is your sampling strategy. In qualitative research, sampling operates according to a purposive rationale – in other words, you select people on purpose because they can provide insight and in-depth understanding to your research. The logic that underlies qualitative sampling is very different from that required for quantitative research, where participants should be selected randomly in large numbers to enable statistical generalisation. The very things that 'would be "bias" in statistical sampling, and therefore a weakness, become intended focus in qualitative sampling, and therefore a strength' (Patton, 2002: 230). Interviewees are deliberately selected because they can offer 'information-rich' data.

The idea of sampling from your population 'implies that selections other than the ones you have made would have been possible, and this means that you need to have and to demonstrate a clear sense of rationale for your choices' (Mason, 2002: 122). If you have a large potential pool of participants in your population, you can draw on one of the common sampling strategies outlined in Table 4.1 to help guide your selection. Use this table to define your interview sample. These sampling strategies are not mutually exclusive, and you might find you adopt elements of snowball sampling with criterion or opportunistic sampling. (For a more comprehensive guide to sampling strategies in qualitative research, we recommend Patton, 2002: 230–42.)

Table 4.1 Common sampling strategies in qualitative research

Sampling strategy	What does this entail?	When might you use this?	Potential problems
Snowball sampling	Asking those who have been previously interviewed to identify other participants	This is a common method in qualitative research. When you are studying a programme or an organisation, there is often a limited number of key people who have the information you need, and recommendations to speak to these people are made. It is also a useful strategy when your population is hard to access, and an introduction via a trusted contact/gatekeeper aids recruitment	You may end up with participants with very similar characteristics, or some participants may never be suggested because the gatekeeper does not know about them or want them to be interviewed Also be mindful of the ethics of contacting people, who have been referred to you, out of the blue. Ideally, the person who refers someone they know should get in contact with them first and ask them if it is OK if you get in touch with them
Criterion sampling	Selecting those people/cases that meet a predetermined criterion. Sometimes these parameters are set to match socio-demographic categories	This strategy can be useful if you want to make comparisons within your sample and you need participants with diverse characteristics to make this comparison	Inclusion and exclusion criteria must be carefully decided beforehand. This will not produce a representative sample but will allow you to have diversity in your sample
Theoretical sampling	Selecting interviewees based on their potential contribution to developing theory	This approach is advocated in grounded theory (see Charmaz, 2014; Mason, 2002). It is an iterative process of an initial sampling, followed by analysis of the data which then informs the selection of subsequent participants, with the purpose of refining emerging concepts and theories	This approach requires more time than other approaches because analysis needs to be factored into the process. This might make it harder to predict the resources needed for this strategy

(Continued)

Table 4.1 (Continued)

Sampling strategy	What does this entail?	When might you use this?	Potential problems
Opportunistic or emergent sampling	Making on-the-spot decisions about who to interview whilst in the process of data collection	This approach allows you to take advantage of unforeseen opportunities after your fieldwork has begun. It is a good strategy when little is known about a phenomenon and the researcher wants to take advantage of what they learn in a setting before selecting participants	You cannot know in advance who you will be interviewing, which may make planning for interviews more difficult and could cause problems with an ethical review board
Convenience sampling	Participants are selected because they are easy to access	This strategy might be useful for preliminary or pilot research to test out your interview guide, for example	This is not a strategic or purposeful approach, so it is the least rigorous and defensible strategy

How many interviews do I need to do?

We are often asked how many interviews will be enough. If you are conducting an interview project as part of your university studies, it's a good idea to check with the dissertation module leader about expectations regarding the number of interviews, as these will vary by institution and discipline. Gathering large samples in qualitative studies is usually inappropriate because of the amount of time it takes to recruit, conduct and analyse the data you have collected (Brinkmann and Kvale, 2015; Ritchie et al., 2014). Unlike a quantitative study which is all about achieving a large sample size, in qualitative studies the careful selection of an appropriate sample is what is needed. More interviewees do not equal better science in qualitative projects. It makes little sense to collect lots of interviews and then not properly use the data because you have run out of time to analyse it. It is better to do fewer interviews but to plan and conduct them well.

We are sure you are still thinking, but how many is enough? There are no rules because the number of interviews needed depends on many factors including your research question, the nature of your population and the richness of the data gathered in each interview. Table 4.2 outlines some of the considerations that can help you determine your sample size at the planning stage.

Table 4.2 Some considerations about sample size

What to consider	The effect on your sample size
How similar are your participants?	If you know your population is very diverse (heterogeneous) in relation to your research issue, you will need to have a large sample to capture this diversity. If your population is very similar (or homogenous), a smaller sample will suffice
How many 'variables' do you want to use to select your participants?	Suppose you want to ensure that men and women from three different age groups are represented in your study: you will need to recruit enough numbers of each category of interviewee to be able to say anything meaningful about these six groups. The more 'variables' or selection criteria you have, the larger your sample size will be
Is your study designed to follow participants over time?	If your study design involves interviewing people on more than one occasion with long intervals in between, it would be recommended to recruit a large sample size. Longitudinal studies suffer from higher levels of participant drop-out than those conducted on a one-shot basis
What resources do you have available?	Each interview takes considerable resources in terms of money and time, so the availability of these will influence your sample size

And we still haven't said how many! This is because once you consider all these factors, as well as how each interview actually occurs in practice (you may have an interview that gives very little data, for instance), it is very difficult to give you a number. Different practitioners have suggested some ball-park figures which you may find useful. For example, Braun and Clarke (2013: 48) suggest 6–10 interviews for a small project, 10–20 interviews for a medium-sized project and over 20 interviews for a large project. Brinkmann and Kvale (2015: 140), meanwhile, suggest that most interview projects will include 15 interviews but that this can vary by +/–10 depending on the time and resources available for the project. Once you are no longer hearing anything different – often termed 'saturation', drawing from grounded theory (Charmaz, 2014) – your sample size is probably sufficient. In a study that tested the idea of theoretical saturation (Guest et al., 2006), the authors found that the majority of themes uncovered in the study with 60 qualitative interviews were found after analysing just six of these interviews, and after 12 interviews few new themes emerged. However, the authors warn against assuming that 6–12 interviews are sufficient to reach theoretical saturation in all cases, for the reasons outlined in Table 4.2.

Rather than focusing on numbers of interviews, it is often better to think about the richness and diversity of the data captured. You need enough data to be able to tell a rich, diverse and nuanced story but not so much that you are unable to process what you have collected or make sense of the complexity within the time you have.

Step 3: Assessing the feasibility of the chosen sampling strategy

Assessing the feasibility of your approach to sampling is an ongoing process rather than a discrete step, but we have included it as a distinct step so that its importance is not overlooked. You will notice in Figure 4.1 that we recommend you revisit step 3 as you start recruiting your sample at step 4.

Box 4.1

Stop & Reflect

Identifying potential sampling problems

Take a moment now to think about all the things that might influence whether you can continue with your intended sampling strategy from step 2. How might you overcome these hurdles?

Some of the things you might have thought about are: whether you know anyone within your sample or have any contacts who can aid you in recruiting your sample. It is always possible to cold-call potential participants and advertise for participants, but this can raise ethical and practical hurdles. It can be helpful to identify a key informant or gatekeeper to help with recruitment. We will talk more about this in step 4.

You might have a very tight budget and timetable (as is often the case with student projects) so an approach, like theoretical sampling, that requires more of these resources may not be feasible.

If you are studying a hard-to-reach or an at-risk population, your safety as a researcher visiting these locations to recruit interviewees may limit who you can access, or the individuals you want to talk to may be protected themselves. You may find you need to rethink your sampling strategy or even your research focus.

Although it might be a good idea to sample according to the criterion of geographical location to see how an experience differs in different places, you may not have the time or money (or capability, given social distancing restrictions, for example) to travel to multiple sites to conduct interviews. In this case, a Zoom/Skype or telephone interview might be appropriate as an alternative. You will, however, need to bear in mind that virtual interviews can be shorter than face-to-face ones, and it is often more of a challenge to develop rapport. Another option is to narrow your locations to 2–3 sites so you can visit them yourself.

Some hurdles can be overcome whilst others are more difficult. In writing this book at the time of the COVID-19 pandemic, we are seeing many student projects turning to the virtual space to recruit and conduct interviews. This context makes clear how important it is to adapt your strategy and continually assess how you might access participants throughout your project. Moving interview projects online requires thought about adapting your recruitment criteria and restricting participation only to those with access to technology and webcams, for example (Salmons, 2012).

Once you start looking at the practicalities of selecting an interview sample, you may realise that your project is too risky, challenging or time-consuming for the scale of project you want to conduct. At the point of submitting an ethical review (see Chapter 5), some of these risks to the researcher and participants may be highlighted. It is a good idea, at this planning stage, to consider whether you need to make adjustments to your sampling approach. For example, rather than using an opportunistic sample to interview drug addicts on the street, work with a local counselling service to identify potential participants who could be interviewed with the help of this service.

Activity 4.1

Develop your sampling frame

Follow steps 1–3 to develop a sampling frame for your interview project. Make a note of any potential problems that you think you might encounter in trying to recruit these participants and your strategies to overcome them. Don't forget to keep an ongoing record of the decisions you have taken along the way in your reflexive journal. It is so easy to forget why you chose to do something the way you did when it comes to writing up your methodology section.

Step 4: Making initial contact with potential participants

This step is the most challenging because it involves finding and encouraging people to be interviewed for your project, which, in a world where people are busy and time-poor, can be difficult. We have broken down this step into four key sections with frequently asked questions from students alongside them.

(i) Locating participants

The first challenge you will face is in locating potential participants, finding out how you can reach them physically or virtually and where/how they might be most receptive to an interview request. Box 4.2 lists some of the strategies you could use to locate participants for your interview study.

Your approach will vary according to who your potential participants are. For example, when conducting research with organisational representatives or elites/experts, it makes sense to first contact them through their institutional affiliation. This is because you will likely be interviewing them about their professional role or expertise rather than their leisure or family life. Such interviewees are easy to contact through an institutional email or are searchable via social media such as LinkedIn and Twitter. Try to guess the email address of the person you want to interview rather than send an email to a generic address. Often, with a bit of detective work you can make an educated guess at the email by searching for the format that an organisation uses for its email addresses (often, it is firstname.lastname@organisation.com, or some variant of this). Alternatively, a PhD student that Katy worked with had great success in contacting interviewees using LinkedIn messages by upgrading to a professional account for a small fee for a couple of months.

For interviewees who are being interviewed about personal experiences or leisure activities, contacting them via their workplace is less appropriate. As noted in Chapter 3, when preparing your interview guide, it is often a good idea to spend time in the places where your participants hang out to learn about the things that matter to them. This might involve spending time at a community centre, attending public meetings, joining a volunteer network or engaging with participants via social media groups. Rubin and Rubin (2012) recommend using these opportunities as a way of gaining trust and finding points of shared interest – stress your passion for gardening or your experience of being a parent as a way of gaining their trust. Being interested in your potential participants and engaging with them on a genuine level are important. People are often more willing to talk to you if they have previously met you or have some personal connection to you, or a mutual acquaintance.

Box 4.2

Some strategies for locating potential participants

- Emailing letters or talking directly with potential participants
- Hanging out in locations where you know your participants will be and making contact with them informally, or by volunteering in community activities
- Giving a talk about your research to the group you are interested in recruiting from
- Finding a trusted insider or gatekeeper who can introduce the research to potential participants on your behalf
- Partnering with an organisation or a charity and using their networks to meet people and advertise the project

- Putting up flyers in public spaces and in places you know your participants will be, such as university campuses, libraries, community centres, doctors' surgeries, places of worship, and shops
- Placing advertisements in local newspapers or newsletters of organisations
- Emailing notices about your research to relevant listservs or email lists, with the list owner's permission
- Using social media sites to promote the research to relevant groups (seek permission from group administrators before posting adverts).

(ii) Working with gatekeepers

To aid your recruitment, it is often a good idea to find someone who knows your participants and can help grant you access. Such a person is often referred to as a 'gatekeeper' (King et al., 2019) or 'key informant' (Barbour, 2014). It is common in ethnographic research to enlist the help of a trusted member of a closed or hard-to-access community. Even with qualitative interview research in communities or organisations, it is helpful to have a champion or spokesperson for your research, who can help create opportunities for you to meet potential participants. For example, in a project on recycling in Shropshire, Katy found a keen composter who ran courses for residents on how to manage food and garden waste at home. This individual was very helpful in introducing her to other keen recyclers in the area. Gatekeepers, who are well liked and respected in a community, can really help the researcher to gain the trust of potential participants. In some cases, access to these communities would be impossible for researchers without the help of such trusted individuals.

Box 4.3

Stop & Reflect

Gatekeepers

Gatekeepers are invaluable for providing access to potential participants in some research projects, but what might be some of the disadvantages of using gatekeepers for recruitment?

You may have thought about the time it might take to gain the trust of the gatekeeper and how you will encourage them to help you; and about the potential for your gatekeeper to control the access you have to participants, which may influence the range of experiences explored within your sample.

Getting your gatekeeper on-side will often involve some expectations of compensation, possibly in the form of access to research findings. It could also be that you offer to volunteer for an organisation or a community group as a thank you to the gatekeeper for aiding recruitment on your study. You might offer to share your findings by running a free workshop for the group, or even a training session that could be useful to their organisation members. Be clear about the level of involvement that a gatekeeper will have in the study, however. This should usually be restricted to aiding with recruitment only, because you do not want your potential participants to worry about the impartiality of the study or that what they say will be reported back to the gatekeeper.

You must reflect carefully on the potential biases that using gatekeepers can introduce into your research. Gatekeepers control who you have access to, and it is important to think about whether some potential participants are not suggested because the gatekeeper does not want the researcher to talk to them or simply because the gatekeeper does not know them. In a project about care home residents, Bethany found that one of the care home managers discouraged her from interviewing certain residents and Bethany needed to consider why these residents were not chosen to speak about their experiences in the home. Of course, she had to abide by the care home manager's wishes because of the environment she was researching within, but she made notes in her reflexive journal about this so they could be included in any accounts of methodology she later wrote about the project. In the example of the recycling project, Katy's gatekeeper was a keen recycler and could only really help her to access other keen recyclers. As the project was about experiences of recycling in general in this county, she had to use other tactics (adverts in local community centres and snowballing techniques) to find participants with differing experiences and attitudes towards this practice.

Another point to consider, especially within organisational research, is where within the power hierarchy your gatekeeper sits. Is your gatekeeper a member of senior management and will potential participants feel obligated to participate in your project because their manager has asked them to? If so, you may compromise ethical protocols by using this gatekeeper, and care must be taken to inform potential participants that their involvement in the research is completely voluntary and that any data collected will not be fed back to senior management. Senior management will also need to be made aware of these principles and their involvement in the research should be for recruitment purposes only.

(iii) Encouraging people to participate

Once you have decided on a route for locating participants, you then need to think about how you will encourage people to take part in, or help you with, your research. There are so many competing demands on people's time, so you need a convincing reason for someone to give that time to you for an interview. Often, just saying you are a student in need of help with your studies is a compelling reason for many people to give time to you. Also, if you have an introduction from a trusted gatekeeper or mutual contact then social obligations to that pre-existing contact might be enough to secure a positive response for an interview.

Connecting your research to a higher social goal, such as learning about how a programme functions so that it can be improved for future users or contributing to the evidence base around a serious social problem, might persuade people to agree to an interview for altruistic motives. Be careful not to over-promise what your research and a participant's involvement will achieve. For example, suppose your project was about exploring the experiences of those in receipt of welfare benefits in order to improve the system. You would need to emphasise the potential for the research to improve the system for others in the future, rather than promise that participation in your study will directly improve the financial and social situation of your participant.

Box 4.4 offers some examples of the sorts of things you can highlight, or do, to encourage people to participate in your research. Do remember that an interview can be an enjoyable and productive experience for the interviewee as it can offer them a period of time to talk freely and openly about an issue that they are passionate about or have direct experience of. Although incentives are often offered, stress to potential participants that you are really interested in what they have to say, and you want to listen to their ideas. It can be flattering for a participant to be asked to be involved in a research project.

Box 4.4

Strategies for encouraging people to participate in an interview project

- Tell them you are a student in need of help
- Offer to work for them for free
- Organise a free event or training session for them
- Share your research findings with them
- Highlight the ways your research might be used for a valued social goal
- Offer a meal, drinks or snacks when you meet participants
- Give a small thank you gift such as a box of chocolates or bottle of wine
- Offer some monetary incentive (e.g. a gift voucher, entry to a prize draw)
- Offer to make a charitable donation
- Cover reasonable out-of-pocket expenses for travel and subsistence.

How do I write a contact letter to a potential participant?

Students often ask us how they can approach an organisation or someone they do not know, using a contact letter to ask them to participate. You will likely have to provide a sample contact letter to submit alongside your ethical approval forms, so it is something to think about early on in your planning. Be aware that some participants can be suspicious of researchers, especially if they have had a bad previous experience of talking to a journalist, for instance. One of the key features of an introductory contact letter is to establish your credibility as a legitimate researcher.

A well-crafted contact letter should be clearly written (free from typos and jargon) and inform a potential participant about your project, giving enough detail that they can make an informed decision about whether and how to participate in your study. In this letter, you should set out for your potential participant why they might want to take part. The checklist in Box 4.5 lists the information that should appear in an introductory letter to a potential participant, and an example introductory letter is provided in Box 4.6.

Box 4.5

Checklist of what should appear in a contact letter to a potential participant

- Who you are and the organisation you represent (from your institutional email address and using an institutional letter head, if possible)
- The name of the funder of the research, if appropriate
- What your project is about and why the participant might be interested in this
- Why you have contacted this person (maybe via a gatekeeper's recommendation or because you know they have expertise in this area)
- What participation will involve
- The potential benefits of participation or incentives to participate
- How the research information collected will be used (remember ethical protocols like anonymisation and the right to withdraw) – this information can be included on a separate participant information sheet rather than providing lots of detail in the introductory email/letter
- Next steps if they are interested in participating
- Your contact details and, if appropriate, the contact details of your supervisor (email address and telephone number)
- A thank you to them for considering your request.

Box 4.6

Example of a contact letter

Dear [name of participant],

I am a researcher from the University of Essex and I am involved in a project that is exploring educational resources for sustainable development, such as those produced by [name of participant's organisation]. This small-scale project has been funded by the British Academy and is entitled 'Educating young people as sustainable citizen-consumers'.

I am writing to ask whether you would be willing to take part in this research by talking to me about the creation of [name of relevant educational resource]. I am keen to learn how and why you went about devising these resources, what you hope these sorts of educational interventions will achieve for sustainability goals, and to gain your thoughts on how best to engage young people as sustainable citizen-consumers. It is hoped that the project will contribute policy-relevant information about the sorts of sustainability messages communicated to young people and whether there are opportunities for sharing best practice. Every attempt will be made to communicate the findings of this research to relevant practitioner audiences.

Your participation would involve a face-to-face interview at a time and place convenient to you. I expect that the interview will take no longer than an hour. With your permission, the interview will be digitally recorded (audio). Should you choose to participate, please be aware that your comments will be treated confidentially, and you will have access to a copy of your transcript and a final research report. For more information about the project and your participation, please see the attached participant information sheet.

I would be very grateful if you could let me know whether you are interested in taking part by either replying to this email (katy.wheeler@essex.ac.uk) or contacting me by phone (+44 (0)1206 873061). If you require any further information, please do not hesitate to contact me.

Thank you for taking the time to consider this request.

Best wishes,
Dr Katy Wheeler (Senior Lecturer in Sociology, University of Essex)

How do I advertise for participants?

Another key mechanism for recruiting participants is a flyer or an advertisement which might be distributed in a public place, through social media or via a newsletter. As with the contact letter, an example advert will need to be supplied at the point of ethical review. In terms of the content, an advert needs to provide much of the same information as in a contact letter, but it cannot be as detailed as a contact letter and won't be tailored to the individual. You might want to set up a website so that interested participants can check out you and your project in more detail.

We recommend using eye-catching fonts or images to grab the reader's attention (particularly for flyers), alongside a short blurb about the project and any potential benefits of participation. If you are looking for people with specific experiences or characteristics, you should state this clearly on the advert. You might want to devise a simple screening questionnaire to sample from those who reply (thinking about ensuring a diversity of characteristics or experiences for your sample) rather than relying on a first-come basis. A example advert that Katy used for her project on consumption work is provided in Box 4.7.

Box 4.7

Example recruitment advert

Researchers from the University of Essex are searching for ten Essex households (from Rochford and Chelmsford) to participate in a research project about recycling, food preparation and the setting up of computer equipment.

We want to know if people are now required to do more work than previously in order to buy and use goods and services. It is likely that over your lifetime, you have experienced changes in how you buy and dispose of consumer goods. Booking holidays online yourself or assembling flat-pack furniture are examples of things we are expected to do now that used to be done as paid employment by travel agents or furniture makers. Our project explores this 'consumption work'.

Your participation would involve two stages: first, we would like to meet with you for a face-to-face interview lasting for about an hour at the time of your choosing; second, we will provide you with a diary sheet (and in some cases a disposable camera) and ask you to keep a record of your 'consumption work' during the course of a normal week. Your participation is voluntary and you can withdraw at any time, without giving a reason.

The research is being undertaken by Professor Miriam Glucksmann and her research team based at the University of Essex (see www.essex.ac.uk/sociology/research/divlab).

It is funded by the European Research Council. We offer a £20 gift voucher to thank you for your participation. If you are interested in taking part, please contact Katy Wheeler (katy.wheeler@essex.ac.uk or 01206 873061).

Do I have to pay participants?

Students often ask whether they need to pay participants to encourage them to participate in their projects. Often, ethical review boards discourage or limit payment because of fears that monetary incentives might coerce people to participate. Paying for participants could undermine altruistic motives for participation and create an expectation that interviewees have to tell the interviewer what they want to hear rather than feeling they can speak freely. However, offering payments adds value to the time involved in contributing to a research project and can make research more inclusive by providing recompense for travel and childcare costs, for example. Providing monetary incentives to research participants is common in social science research, but remains controversial (Head, 2009). It will depend on the characteristics of your sample – in organisational research where you are interviewing someone during work hours, payment is likely to be inappropriate, whereas in interviewing a lone mother about her childcare experiences during an evening or weekend, as in Head's research, payment was necessary to encourage participants to come forward.

We have had different experiences of offering incentives in our research, both positive and negative. Bethany often conducts very long interviews and struggles to know what is an appropriate thank you gift. During her PhD, she had limited funds and so offered a £5 book token to each participant. She had very different responses to these gifts – one participant started crying when presented with the token, whilst another threw the token over his shoulder without looking at it. She thought, 'if someone is opening their life experiences to you, can a gift card ever compensate them for this?' This was the sort of thing that she reflected on in her analysis of the interviews overall, but it highlights the importance of thinking carefully about the best ways to compensate people for the time they offer when participating in research projects.

Activity 4.2

Think about incentives

You are conducting research into drug use in your local area. You interview 10 homeless substance users. What would be an appropriate incentive for this population?

Our advice is that if you do want to offer a payment to participants, it should be kept relatively small (£10–£20) and practically focused (such as a gift voucher or book token). As a student, you may not have funds to offer each participant, so there are other ways to say thank you for participation, such as those outlined in Box 4.4.

Activity 4.3

Design recruitment materials

Using the advice provided above, either design a recruitment advertisement or draft an introductory contact letter for your interview study. Think carefully about

(Continued)

how you will represent your research to potential participants and what types of incentives you will offer. Is your incentive appropriate for the population you are trying to recruit from?

Optional group-based extension: Share your advert or contact letter with a class member and ask for their feedback. Together, discuss the potential advantages and disadvantages of using incentives to encourage participation in your project.

(iv) Being persistent

Initial attempts to contact participants may not result in as many interviews as you had hoped for. This is completely normal, and you therefore must build enough time into your planning to allow for delays at this stage. Sometimes people are not deliberately ignoring your request for an interview but have just not got around to replying to you. If you have contacted a named individual by email or letter, try to make contact again 1–2 weeks after the initial letter. You might want to call them on the phone as it is harder to ignore a request that comes via this route. If you do call, remember that you should be ready to give a summary of your research and know when you have free time to meet (more on this at step 5). If, after a second or third attempt, you have still had no reply, it is probably a good idea to move on to a different individual. Participants have the right to refuse participation in your study and if they have ignored repeated requests, you should respect their right to be left alone. Case study 4.1 gives an account of what Katy calls 'systematic persistence' in her search for interviewees for a project on environmental activism.

Case study 4.1

Systematic persistence

In a project, which involved researching how European civil society organisations engage in lobbying activities, Katy developed a strategy for securing 'expert' interviewees. Whilst civil society organisations are more open to being interviewed than many other expert interviewees (such as those in the private sector), they were busy people who did not often respond to unsolicited emails. This is a problem many students encounter and the key to recruiting interviewees is systematic persistence.

Katy began by crafting a well-written introductory email that established her credibility as a legitimate researcher – this is a good starting point. Katy researched the names of the representatives that she wanted to secure interviews with and did her best to guess the correct email address rather than send it to a generic account. The email came from her institutional university account and attached to the email was an introduction to the research project which was printed on university-headed paper and included information about what participation would involve, as well as when Katy hoped to conduct the interviews when in Brussels. After contacting 15 representatives this way, she received a handful of responses. The remaining interviewees were emailed a second time, about 10 days after the original email, asking again if they would be interested in taking part. This yielded an additional couple of responses.

Any outstanding interviewees were then called on the telephone about a week after the second email. Sometimes it took several calls before Katy got to speak to the right person. Once located, Katy explained who she was and why she wanted to talk to them, highlighting that she had sent several emails to them previously about their participation. She found it handy to have the dates of those sent emails as often the person would be in front of their computer and was able to scroll through and locate that contact. In some cases, the email had ended up in a junk folder, so the participant had not seen it before. The phone call worked to secure the interview as participants were often willing to set a date there and then, and in some cases to suggest alternative people who might usefully be contacted to take part in the research.

Katy puts her success in recruiting interviewees in this project (and subsequent projects) down to her systematic persistence. It was the repeated efforts to contact potential interviewees through different mechanisms, which together worked. Of course, there are always those who do not reply or do not want to take part (which is their right); but do not give up until you have done everything you can to speak to the person you are interested in interviewing.

If you are relying on adverts and flyers rather than direct letters/emails, you should expect that replies will take time. You may need to get more involved in local events, engage in online forums and/or attend the places your participants will be to try to foster some more personalised contacts. For example, in order to encourage Fairtrade supporters to agree to interviews, Katy attended a range of Fairtrade Town events so that she could meet people face to face and explain more about her research. In Head's (2009) research on lone mothers, she adapted her incentives and offered £10 for participation which led to more interest from lone mothers, as well as a willingness by family support workers to allow her access to groups to recruit from.

Step 5: Securing the interview

Once you receive a reply or response to your letter or advertisement, the next stage is to secure the interview. You will want to act quickly to schedule a meeting at a time and place that is of mutual convenience. Make sure you have your diary in front of you when talking to a potential participant so that you can easily find a mutually convenient time. You should be as flexible as possible, fitting in around your participant's schedule.

If you have recruited via a flyer or advertisement and have no prior connection with the interviewee through a gatekeeper or mutual acquaintance, think carefully about the location of your interview. Remember your own personal safety and meet in a public place (like a café or park) during daylight hours, or with a friend if this is not possible. You may decide to conduct the interview online if you are concerned about visiting an interviewee at their home in the evening.

It is a good idea to confirm the agreed place and time for the interview by letter or calendar invitation so that the interviewee has a record of this information. The day before the interview, a quick call or email checking the interviewee is still available and stating you are looking forward to talking to them, will remind interviewees of the agreed meeting time. Katy has learned from experience that this courtesy is important after turning up for interviews where the interviewees had forgotten the appointment.

What if an interviewee wants to do the interview on the phone, online or by email?

You might find that your interviewee agrees to be interviewed but wants to do the interview straight away on the phone, or over a video-conferencing service (like Zoom or Skype) or by email. You will need to decide how to handle this situation. We definitely recommend not doing the interview straight away unless there really is no other option. It is better to try to schedule the interview at a time when both you and the interviewee are fully prepared, and you have both cleared your schedules for this purpose.

In terms of whether to conduct the interview via the phone, online or by email, this will be a judgement call. We both prefer face-to-face interviews and these have been described as the 'gold standard' in terms of validity and rigour in qualitative research (Deakin and Wakefield, 2014). Face-to-face interviews enable you to better build a rapport and follow up on visual cues, like body language. But online or telephone interviews can overcome problems of scheduling and allow you to include people who are unwilling to be interviewed face to face (see Chapter 2 for the key advantages and disadvantages of online synchronous interviews). They are an acceptable 'plan b' and some researchers have argued that they can generate data that is as good as face-to-face interactions (Holt, 2010; Janghorban et al., 2014; Weller, 2017). In the wake of the COVID-19 pandemic, it has become commonplace for people to conduct varied social interactions via remote methods. At the time of writing, it seems likely that we are on the brink of a sea-change shift towards the normalisation of online communications. So, we think it highly likely that online synchronous interviews will become more commonplace in future research projects than they have been in the past.

Email interviews that use a synchronous chat facility might also be an acceptable alternative if both the researcher and the interviewee are comfortable communicating quickly using this medium. However, when someone asks for an email interview, it is our experience that they expect you to send them a list of questions they will answer in their own time, with minimal opportunities for follow-up questions from you. This then becomes more like a qualitative survey rather than an interview and the responses you receive will not be as rich and detailed as those you can gather through face-to-face, online video or telephone interviews, which will influence your analysis.

How many interviews can I do in a day?

If you have the luxury of lots of time and you do not need to travel far to conduct an interview, allowing a whole day for each interview is ideal. However, we appreciate you will often have a limited period in which to conduct your interviews and it is likely you'll have to do more than one interview in a day. We would recommend you schedule about two interviews in a day, and certainly no more than three. Even though your interviews may take just an hour or so to conduct, they require a lot of mental energy and it is not a good idea to do an interview when you are tired. Also, you will want to leave enough time between interviews to allow for instances where interviews may overrun, or to travel to the next interview location. If you are working in a specific location (maybe a different country or part of the country) and have just a few days in this location to conduct all your interviews, do not fully book yourself because an interviewee may unexpectedly need to postpone and you will want to make sure you can accommodate this. Also, other relevant people to speak to may be recommended by your interviewees and there should be space in your schedule for this type of opportunistic sampling.

Top tip summary

- Identify who will most likely be able to offer useful and relevant data for your interview study. These people are your study population.
- Only interview your friends if they have the necessary experience or relevant knowledge to help you address your research question.

(Continued)

- Choose from the different sampling strategies (see Table 4.1) to help you select individuals from your population to form a sampling frame.
- Rather than focus on how many interviews you need, make sure that you have enough data to develop a diverse and complex story but not so much that you cannot process it all in the time you have.
- You should be continually assessing your sampling strategy for feasibility and make changes where necessary. Be sure to record all decisions in your reflexive journal.
- Gatekeepers or trusted insiders are invaluable for accessing potential participants but be aware that a gatekeeper's interests and agenda might limit who you recruit and what they feel comfortable saying.
- A clear contact letter or recruitment advert should introduce your research to potential participants and give them enough information to make an informed choice about whether to participate. See Boxes 4.5, 4.6 and 4.7 for guidance on how to prepare these resources.
- There are many ways you can encourage people to take part in your research project (see Box 4.4), but persistence is often the key to securing an interview.
- Be flexible when you schedule your interviews at a time and place that is convenient for the interviewee; but be sure to also consider researcher safety when organising interviews with people you do not know.

5

THINK ETHICALLY

Learning objectives

On completing this chapter, you should be able to:

- Recognise key ethical considerations when conducting qualitative research
- Develop an awareness and sensitivity to ethical challenges in the research process
- Apply appropriate strategies for securing informed, valid consent from participants
- Recognise that data can have a longer lifespan than the research project which creates it
- Defend any ethical decisions made during the research process.

This chapter will help you understand and think through the key ethical challenges of conducting qualitative interviews, using real-life scenarios and case studies drawn from our own research experiences. We will take you through the process of obtaining informed and valid consent from participants, and provide example consent and information sheets. Elements of the consent process will be explained, such as the long-term strategies for data storage, mechanisms of withdrawal, limits to confidentiality in small sample groups, and the use of real names versus pseudonyms. We look at whether written or verbal consent is appropriate, and how this choice needs to be matched to the requirements of the participants. You will be encouraged to think about the life cycle of the data project and how you can promote the full usage of your materials if you gain the right level of consent. Throughout the chapter, we will show you some examples of our own ethical challenges and how these were dealt with.

Ethics – why bother?

You might be thinking, 'why should I bother with ethics? This is the boring bit of the research process and an unnecessarily bureaucratic burden.' Well, we are here to convince you that being aware of the ethical issues in your research is an integral part of the research process (and can actually be quite interesting). Good ethical practice should not be viewed as a cumbersome process deliberately designed to catch you out, but rather as a vital way of ensuring the dignity and safety of everyone involved in the research.

Notorious cases

Today, in the majority of established education and research institutions, any research that is conducted must be submitted to an ethics committee. This might take place at a departmental level, a school level, a university level, or even a wider institutional or disciplinary level, such as an NHS ethics committee (in the UK).

There is good reason to submit your work to a committee and why as researchers we should 'think ethically'. Prior to ethical procedures being formalised by universities, there was a series of infamous studies which attracted negative attention for their ethical practices. Box 5.1 contains three of the most renowned cases which took place in the 1970s, and one study in which the fieldwork took place in the 2000s.

Box 5.1

Notorious case examples

Case 1: In 1973 David Rosenhan published the article 'On being sane in insane places'. In this study, Rosenhan, along with his team of experimenters, 'pseudo-patients', feigned hallucinations so they could covertly gain access to psychiatric hospitals to test the reliability of mental health diagnoses. The study posed a number of ethical challenges, including the deception of the hospital staff and other patients who had no opportunity to consent to or withdraw from the study. Rosenhan created a public mistrust in the hospital admissions system which deterred those who genuinely needed treatment from seeking it. He also failed in his duty of care towards his staff – his group of experimenters – who he put into positions of potential harm in the hospital.

Case 2: In 1974 Stanley Milgram conducted a series of experiments which culminated in his publication *Obedience to Authority*. One of his most well-known experiments set out to test how far people would go in obeying an instruction given by someone in authority. Milgram put the unknowing study volunteers in a 'teacher' role who were then asked, by an 'experimenter' (who was an actor), to administer potentially lethal electric shocks to a 'learner' (who was also an actor) if they got the answers to questions in a test wrong. The experimenter encouraged the 'teacher' to continue administering the shocks, even when the 'learner' feigned screams and begged for the 'teacher' to stop. Some of the key ethical challenges of this study included the deception in play where the research participant believed they were really shocking another person; the stress and psychological harm done to participants; and finally, lack of the right to withdraw from the study because the study participant 'teacher' was told they must continue with the shock punishments.

Case 3: Laud Humphreys' *Tearoom Trade: Impersonal Sex in Public Places* (1970) is one of the most notorious studies of its time. Humphreys conducted a covert ethnographic study of anonymous male homosexual encounters in public toilets in a practice known as the tearoom trade. It was a public space and he was allowed there, but the people who were being studied did not know he was a researcher. In order to infiltrate their activities without them realising, he played the role of a 'watch queen' or voyeur. It would have been rather awkward to ask them for an interview or to complete a survey in that particular situation, so Humphreys' solution was to follow the men, take note of their licence plates, find their personal details through police records, then change identity and pose as a researcher conducting a 'health survey'. He conducted this research project with great sacrifice to his own personal integrity and brought his discipline into disrepute. This particular study highlighted the increasing intrusiveness of social research at that time. It was a particularly deceptive form of research practice, which Humphreys argued was justified due to the fact that it would have been impossible to gather the data any other way. Even more concerning was the fact that homosexual acts, at that time, were a crime in most of the USA, and had any of the identities of the men involved been revealed it could have led to social stigmatisation, loss of family or job and even arrest and imprisonment.

Case 4: Alice Goffman spent six years conducting an immersive urban ethnographic study of a Black community of high social deprivation in West Philadelphia. This research began with her undergraduate dissertation fieldwork and extended into her PhD. During this period, she closely observed a group of young Black men, whom she named the '6th Street Boys', even moving into their neighbourhood to try to better understand their lives and their community.

(Continued)

Whilst observing, she was witness to their criminal activities, misdemeanours and legal entanglements. Her resulting book, *On the Run: Fugitive Life in an American City (2014)* was published to high acclaim and was hailed a new ethnographic classic text.

However, along with her success, came a great deal of scrutiny of her methods, her ethical decisions and the veracity of her written account.

First, her positionality was scrutinised. Should a young, White, middle-class female, from an academically prominent family, be the best placed person to represent youth from a disadvantaged Black community? Her critics have argued that her White-gaze portrayal of 'hypercriminalized Black men' and 'hypersexualized Black women' were harmful narratives of that community (see Flaherty, 2017). Second, she gives an account in her book of her own entanglements with illegal activities whilst in the position of a participant observer, including driving a getaway car for the group of gun-carrying young men as they sought revenge for the murder of their friend. She put herself in significant danger and implicated herself in illegal activity. Finally, there have been debates about the truth of her accounts. Some of the stories she writes about have inconsistencies in them and do not hold up well to detailed scrutiny. However, as Goffman destroyed her field notes in an attempt to protect her participants, it is impossible to evaluate whether this evidence supports her claims.

Thinking ethically

In order to think ethically, you need to consider three key areas:

1. How can I protect my research participants?
2. How can I protect myself as a researcher?
3. How can I protect my field of research for future researchers?

House (1990: 158) argued that ethical research involves three principles: (1) *mutual respect*, which means understanding each other's aims and interests, not damaging your participant's self-esteem, and not being condescending; (2) *non-coercion and non-manipulation*, which refer to not using force or threats, or leading others to cooperate when it is against their interests; and (3) *support for democratic values and institutions*, which refers to a commitment to equality and liberty and to working against oppression and subjugation.

It is not enough to simply learn ethical principles, but rather to be an ethically responsible qualitative interviewer you need to learn how to make judgements on the situations you find yourself in. (See the later section on Situation Ethics for more detail on this.)

Ethics in the research life cycle

Thinking about ethics is not a discrete, singular stage of your research process. It is not just about filling in a form and having your work approved by the ethics committee. Rather, you will need to consider the ethical dimensions of your research throughout the duration of your project.

Box 5.2

Ethics through the research life cycle

- Design of the research – how will your research question contribute to understanding and improving the human situation of those involved? Are there any political sensitivities that need to be taken into consideration?
- Sampling and recruiting – how will you select who takes part? How will you encourage people to participate in your study? How should you repay them?
- During the interview – how will you ask questions in a sensitive and respectful manner? How will you manage challenging behaviour in an interview? How will you respond to participants that become distressed?
- Preparing your data – how will you ensure that transcribers maintain the same levels of confidentiality as you have offered to your participants?
- Disseminating your findings – what say will your participants have in how their data is interpreted?
- Archiving your data – do you have permission to archive? How can you control what other people will do with your data?

Ethics committees

In order to help you think through each of these questions at each stage of your research, you should develop an 'ethical protocol' or complete an institutional ethics form (you may need to ask the ethics lead in your department or your supervisor). We do not offer you an example of an ethics form in this chapter because there is huge variation across institutions and the forms and procedures are subject to rapid change. Box 5.3 summarises the key things you will need to consider when preparing your ethics application.

Your ethics form will be submitted to a research ethics committee (REC) in the UK, or an institutional review board (IRB) in the USA. Practice varies across countries so do check with your home country and home institution what processes you need to follow. However, even if the process for gaining ethical approval varies cross-nationally, the basic principles of ethical good practice remain relatively consistent. It is also worth noting that ethics committees are unlikely to approve applications the first time round. They may ask for further clarification on particular issues. Depending on your research, this can be a long (and sometimes frustrating) process. You should take this potential time delay into consideration when planning the timings of your research. Also, if you do not agree with the decision of the committee, you should have the right to defend your approach. This should not be a top-down process but rather one of mutual dialogue. Do not be afraid of approaching your ethics officer for advice prior to submission to a committee.

If you are conducting health research using medical records or conducting interviews with NHS patients in the UK, you will need to follow an even more rigorous ethical protocol and gain approval from a network of committees. Depending on your research focus, and if you are in the UK, you may need to apply through the Integrated Research Application System (IRAS) to the Health Research Authority (2020a) for permission and approval to conduct health and social care research.

Box 5.3

Things to consider for your ethics application

- A summary of your topic
- An outline of your methodology
- Your recruitment strategies
- Whether you will offer reimbursement to participants
- Sensitivities and how they will be managed
- How you will manage issues of confidentiality and anonymity
- How you will inform participants of the right to withdraw from the study
- How you will securely store your data
- What research outputs you plan to produce
- Any issues of personal risk, including travel to the field
- Attaching an information sheet, consent form and interview guide, where appropriate.

Ethical frameworks

Most countries will have ethical frameworks available via their national research councils. These frameworks contain a range of regulations, principles and standards of good ethical practice in research. They may include risk assessment, and health and safety, in addition to the expectations around ethical conduct. They provide a standard of integrity, quality and transparency in the research process. Any application to an ethics committee will be measured against the standards within these ethical frameworks.

In the UK, a number of research bodies have produced ethical frameworks for their members. In the social sciences, these include:

- Economic and Social Research Council (ESRC) ESRC Framework for Research Ethics
- British Sociological Association (BSA) Statement of Ethical Practice
- Social Research Association (SRA) Ethical Guidelines
- British Psychological Society (BPS) Code of Conduct, Ethical Principles and Guidelines.

This is not an exclusive list however, and your own institution may have its own code of conduct based on these frameworks. Any of the above will be a good starting point for developing your ethical practice.

Ethical principles

Box 5.4

Basic ethical principles

- Preventing harm and avoiding risk and exploitation
- Managing the confidentiality of the data and maintaining the anonymity of respondents
- Being respectful and protecting the autonomy of your participants and, if you are working with vulnerable populations, ensuring that you respect their autonomy too
- Offering clarity about the independence of the research and any intended possible uses of the research.

Let us look at each of the basic ethical principles in Box 5.4 in more detail.

Do no harm

Preventing harm, and avoiding risk and exploitation, should take absolute priority in your research. The ethical principle of *beneficence* refers to causing the least risk of harm possible to a participant. In conducting research, you are making private lives public and it is your duty to safeguard your interviewees. Harm can come about in a variety of ways: physical harm, threat to safety, threat to freedom, harm to development or advancement in a position, loss of self-esteem, stress, embarrassment, and invasion of privacy. You need to consider whether any potential harm to a participant outweighs any potential benefits of doing your research.

Activity 5.1

Notorious cases

Look back at the four notorious ethics case examples at the start of this chapter. Do you think the benefits of those research studies outweigh the potential harm to the participants in each case?

Confidentiality and anonymity

Harm can come to participants if you, as the researcher, do not manage the confidentiality of the research data and maintain the anonymity of your respondents. Managing confidentiality in research refers to restricting identifying details and ensuring attributive quotations in publications are not linked to identified participants.

Anonymity refers to the participant's identity not being known outside the research team, and this can be maintained through changing identifying information such as a person's name. This false name is known as a pseudonym. It is important to choose a pseudonym which is not too close to the original name – so you wouldn't want to use Kathleen for Kathryn, for example, as it might give a hint to the identity. However, you also want to keep the name culturally sensitive and age appropriate, as this retains some of the character and authenticity of the individual. You could use a code number to represent the individual, so, for example, BM79 might represent the participant's initials and their birth year. However, be mindful that a code used to represent an individual can be quite depersonalising and may be awkward to read in a narrative account. This would not be recommended in life story interviews where, for example, you really need to get a sense of who the person is.

Some participants might also request you use their real name. Bethany once conducted a life story interview that lasted five hours and, at the end, she reconfirmed the consent procedures reminding her participant that she would change his name. He was quite cross and exclaimed loudly: 'No, this is my story! I want my real name used. My name is MARIO! Please use my name!' Now, when she conducts research, she always asks her participants whether they would like to use their real name or a pseudonym, and if they would like a false name what they would like to call themselves. Asking a participant to choose a name for themselves can also be quite a revealing activity – you might like to read Sasha Roseneil's (2006) paper, 'The ambivalences of Angel's "arrangement": A psychosocial lens on the contemporary condition of personal life', for a more detailed discussion about the implications of someone choosing their own pseudonym. If someone wants to use their real name, always ensure they understand the implications of this and encourage them to consider any potential risks associated with revealing their identity. Also double-check after the interview that the participant is still happy with what they have contributed and that they still want to use their real name.

As a researcher, you should take care not to offer unrealistic guarantees of confidentiality because, under certain circumstances, you may find you are legally obliged to share the data with relevant authorities and services in order to protect someone who is at risk of significant and immediate harm. For instance, in the unlikely event your participant confesses information about a child currently at risk of abuse, or if your participant makes suicidal threats, you may need to break confidentiality. If this is the case, it is best to talk first to your participant about your need to do this.

If you need to work with an external transcribing company, it is good practice to ask them to sign a confidentiality agreement, which includes an agreement not to share any details that they might hear on the audio recordings, and destroying their additional copies of the data once it has been transcribed.

How anonymity might be compromised

When transcribing your interview data, you need to decide when to anonymise the data. If you try to change names as you listen to the recording, you may find that this interrupts your transcription flow and can be very time-consuming. You may want to transcribe your data in an unanonymised form, followed by an anonymisation process. You need to consider the ways identities can be revealed in the data.

Box 5.5

Ways in which anonymity can be compromised

Direct identifiers – this refers to data which directly identifies the participant, for example their name, their telephone number, their address or postcode, or a photo of their face. In face-to-face interviews, this is often not essential research information and is usually only used for administrative purposes such as contacting the participant to make arrangements for their interview. However, if recording an interview online via video conferencing, you may be recording the participant's image in the video as well as the audio recording.

(Continued)

Indirect identifiers – this is where an identity can be revealed by a combination of information points. For example, if your data described a 'female professor in a Sociology department at the University of Essex', you would be narrowing down the identity of your participant to a very small sample so it may be possible to identify that person. In order to anonymise this participant, you could instead write about a 'female professor in a Sociology department at a UK university'. By expanding the geography in this instance (and if the geography is not important to your project), we widen the potential population and conceal their identity.

Outlying information – so if someone has a revealing characteristic because of their age, race, disability, or an interesting feature about their life story, this too can disclose an identity. Similarly, in small community research, participants may know each other and there is a risk of exposure even if pseudonyms are used. If you judge that it will be too difficult to anonymise someone because of their outlying characteristics, it may be better to gain consent to use their data in an unanonymised form, or warn them that although you will do your best to keep their data confidential, this cannot be guaranteed.

Third-party disclosure – if participation is arranged by a third party then anonymity can be compromised. This is something to take into consideration if you are planning to use a snowball sampling technique. Those who are referred for participation may feel obliged to contact the initial recruiter to verify their eligibility criteria for the study. Best practice is also to require the initial recruiter to contact their referred participant themselves, as opposed to the researcher contacting them directly.

Poor data management – there should be clear protocols about who has access to private, identifying information about participants and who does not. Research data which has not been anonymised should be considered confidential and therefore should not be shared with others outside of a research team, unless there is clear consent to share. Take care when labelling your files too, so that you do not inadvertently compromise anonymity by adding a participant name into a file name. Finally, ensure that any signed documents with names on them are kept away from transcripts, and stored securely in a locked cabinet or scanned and stored in a password-protected file on your computer. Any audio or video files collected from recorded video-conferencing calls should be stored with equal care in password-protected digital folders.

Box 5.6

Anonymisation guidelines

- Never disclose personal data, unless you have consent for disclosure
- Apply a reasonable/appropriate level of anonymity
- Maintain maximum meaningful information
- Where possible, replace rather than remove data
- Identifying information may provide context so do not over-anonymise.

Informed consent

Gaining informed consent is a fundamental part of the research process. It refers to the procedure of telling your participants about your research, their role within it, and once they understand this, their willingness to participate.

The British Sociological Association code of ethics states that participants 'enter into an agreement with a researcher voluntarily and without coercion, improper influence or inducements' (BSA Statement of Ethical Practice, 2017).

Informed consent can be gained through a one-off consent process, whereby you tell the participant about the research and then they agree to take part in it. Or it can be gained through process consent, whereby you inform the participant from the outset and they agree, but in addition you seek consent in the mid or later stages of the research process to check that they are still happy with what they are contributing or have contributed. Although process consent means you can be completely assured about the ongoing issue of consent, it can be disruptive to the flow of your interaction. In fact, respondents often open up more on social occasions, once they have forgotten about your presence as a researcher. It is therefore arguable that it is unethical to constantly remind your participant that they are under research enquiry.

It is easy to forget about the process of gaining informed consent when you are interviewing online. It is good practice to send the information sheet and consent form in advance of the interview, asking for the consent to be digitally signed and returned before the interview, and then asking for basic verbal consent in the online meeting.

Written or verbal consent?

Informed consent can be gained through written or verbal agreement. However, it should be noted that, although in some situations verbal consent might be sufficient, most ethics departments in the UK would insist on formal written consent. Most departments will also have a template form for students to use. Whichever

Table 5.1 Comparing written and verbal consent

Written consent	
Advantages	Disadvantages
• Solid legal evidence	• May be off-putting and cumbersome
• May be required by an ethics committee	• May be culturally inappropriate: some cultures are very wary of signing documents, or even asking for a signature may imply distrust
	• Some populations, such as those involved in criminality, may not want to sign anything
• More protection for the researcher	• May not be possible to use with some populations: consider literacy levels and physical ability to complete a form

process is used, it is important to document how consent is gained and any negotiations which take place.

When conducting research online, you may need to send your participants consent forms in a digital format. These could be returned with a typed signature which is then sent from their own email; or you could ask them to sign a digital form through an online platform such as DocuSign.

Consent forms

If gaining written consent from your participants, you should make your consent form simple and fit for purpose. It is best practice to contain more detailed information on an accompanying information sheet and keep the consent form as a series of tick-boxes which demonstrate that the participant agrees to each individual element of the research process.

Box 5.7

Checklist – Things to include on your consent form

- The purpose of the study
- All the possible intended uses of the data
- Their rights as a research participant
- If and how their data will be anonymised
- How the data will be stored
- Consent to archive
- The participant's right to withdraw

Information sheets

The information sheet should accompany your consent form, and ideally a copy of the information sheet should be given to your research participants in advance so that they have time to read through it.

Box 5.8

Checklist – Things to include on your information sheet

- Your name and a very brief biography
- What the research is about
- How long their participation is expected to take

- What method you will be using
- Why the person has been chosen to be involved
- The risks and benefits of participation
- Who to contact for further information or to make a complaint

---

Activity 5.2

Create an information sheet

Create an information sheet on one of the following research topics:

1. The experience of moving into a care home (aimed at care home residents aged over 80 years old)
2. The experience of pet bereavement (aimed at people aged over 18 years old)
3. The experience of being home-schooled during the COVID-19 lockdown (aimed at children aged 5–10 years old).

Consider the following:

- Is your information sheet clear and simple to understand?
- Does it avoid sensitive language?
- Have you included all the relevant information which is mentioned in Box 5.8?
- Do you have to make any adjustments to the sheet to make it accessible to your population?

Mechanisms of withdrawal

Box 5.9

Mechanisms of withdrawal

Participants have a right:

- not to enter the interview in the first instance
- to decline to answer any questions
- to end the interview at any point.

Participants should be made aware of any risks involved and should have the option to leave the interview, even halfway through. Sometimes researchers write: 'you may withdraw from the research at any point without question'. Of course, you may want to offer an open-ended opportunity to withdraw data which has already been contributed, but there could be a high price to pay if a participant decides to withdraw their data after you have already transcribed their interview, or analysed it, or worse still, published their data. You have a couple of options for the wording of a withdrawal statement: (1) you could time-limit the withdrawal and say the participant has a set amount of time (perhaps 2 weeks?) to withdraw from the research; or (2) you could state that any contributions made until the withdrawal may still be used in the research.

Dealing with disagreements

Not only does your participant have the right to withdraw, but as the researcher you also have the right to terminate an interview if you feel uncomfortable or the interview takes a bad turn. You have the right to politely and firmly draw an interview to a close and leave as soon as possible. Sometimes our interviewees make racist, sexist or offensive statements, so is it acceptable to continue with an interview if the participant's views are in such opposition to our own? How would you ethically handle such disagreements? Thwaites (2017: 3) writes:

> Rapport is highly significant to how one and one's participants become located within the research and how one interprets the data: as one begins to 'identify/disidentify, like/dislike, familiarize/etherized [sic] ' (Bott, 2010: 160). This is an issue for all social science researchers, but for feminist researchers it can threaten the ethics of their research process, which is intended to minimise power, empower silenced voices, and treat all participants with the same respect and interest. Equally though, it shows the importance for researchers of not subsuming their full self to the performance of rapport to 'get the data' – particularly if a participant makes comments that are sexist, racist, and so on (Bott, 2010: 167).

How much of your own self-identity and political ideals are you willing to temporarily sacrifice in order to 'get the data' in the face of such disagreements? It is important for the researcher in such situations to locate their own subjectivity within their research and to consider how they develop and maintain rapport with their participants.

The ethics of remuneration

We discussed incentivising participants to participate in Chapter 4. However, there are also ethical implications in paying participants (renumeration). A large incentive could be considered coercion (and an ethics board could reject your application on this basis), which means that participants might only want to take part for the monetary reward as opposed to wanting to take part in your research.

Box 5.10

Vignette of ethical etiquette

You are conducting community-based fieldwork in a small English village. You arrange to interview 78-year-old Jean, in her own home at 5pm on a Sunday. When you arrive, you find that Jean has cooked you some dinner. What do you do?

1. Graciously accept the meal and then interview Jean afterwards
2. Say that it is unethical to be friends, that you cannot accept the meal, then leave immediately
3. Decline the dinner, let her eat her meal and interview her whilst she eats
4. Decline the dinner and leave but then return an hour later to conduct the interview.

Reflection: This is a tricky situation. Although you may feel that accepting a meal from a participant crosses a boundary between your personal and professional lives, you also need to consider the principle of 'do no harm'. A participant might be offended by you declining their meal, especially if they have cooked it for you, so this could cause them harm (perhaps emotionally and financially). However, if you are not hungry and this situation arose, it might be appropriate to make a compromise saying, 'thank you, but I've already eaten, though I wouldn't mind a drink (or small portion), please'. That way you are accepting her hospitality, maintaining the rapport and not offending her.

Data life cycle

'Data often have a longer lifespan than the research project that creates them' (Corti et al., 2014: 17). You may want to revisit your own data in the future in order to form longitudinal comparisons, you may want to make your data available for other researchers to use, or you may be obliged to store your anonymised research data in an institutional repository. Many research ethics committees will request that you destroy ALL your data after your research project has ended. However, this can be challenging. There is no requirement to destroy any anonymised data and you can make a case that it may have research use in the future. However, personal, identifying data, such as the names and addresses of participants, falls under the General Data Protection Regulation (GDPR) (if you are researching outside of the European Union, check your own country's regulations). Personal data can be stored securely for longer than the research project so long as it is only being kept for future research purposes.

Information about the GDPR can be found here: https://gdpr-info.eu.

Most notably, the fifth principle of the GDPR states that:

> Personal data shall be kept in a form which permits identification of data subjects for no longer than is necessary for the purposes for which the personal data are processed; personal data may be stored for longer periods insofar as the personal data will be processed solely for archiving purposes in the public interest, scientific or historical research purposes or statistical purposes subject to implementation of the appropriate technical and organisational measures required by the GDPR in order to safeguard the rights and freedoms of individuals ('storage limitation'). (https://gdpr-info.eu)

If you plan to make your anonymised data available to other researchers beyond your research project, you may want to consider archiving it with an institutional repository or other data archive. Once archived, you will not necessarily be in a position to control how that data will be used by others, so you may need to check your archiving arrangements.

If your archived data is not suitable for immediate release, or if there is any possibility that you could put your participants in a position of harm through archiving their data you may want to put a time-limited partial restriction on it. This is known as an *embargo*.

If there is any possibility you will archive your data, even in the future, you should include this in your consent form. Participants may be wary of this part of the consent process but, with reassurance that their data will be preserved for future generations, they are more likely to agree. Needless to say, if a participant does not agree to this part of the consent process, you should not include their data. Instead, you can archive the rest of the data and completely restrict access to that singular interview.

Writing ethically

Ethics should also be considered in the writing-up process.

Box 5.11

Ethics in the writing process

To help you write ethically, consider the following questions:

- Are your research findings credible, accurate and representative of your participants' views?
- Have you omitted any significant data, and have you offered a justification for that omission?

- Have you avoided discriminatory language?
- Have you acknowledged your research funders?
- Have you been explicit about any conflict of interest?
- Have you used culturally specific words and precise language to describe your participant's identity? Have you reflected the terminology that they use to describe themselves?
- Would you be happy for your participants to read your portrayals of them?
- Have you reflected on your own biases and preconceptions during the research process?

Situation ethics

Now you are coming to the end of this chapter, you will have read about the rules, regulations and procedures regarding ethics. However, when in the field, nothing is certain and ethical guidelines might not anticipate all of the issues that you might face as a researcher. You may find yourself in a situation which you had not planned for, despite all your training. If you are familiar with the basic frameworks of ethics and work in the best interests of your participants, then you may be able to adapt your ethical approach. This adaptable approach is called *situation ethics*, which is a term coined by Joseph Fletcher (1966/1997). His work aimed to show how an act might go against set standards yet remain morally acceptable. He believed ethics should be founded in freedom, love and personal moral responsibility, rather than in authority structures, rules and ideals. He termed this acting purely out of love and goodwill, 'agape'. One of the key principles of situation ethics is that decisions are made on a case-by-case basis, rather than by judging them by a set standard. One way in which you might judge your ethical standards is through the *test of universality* – would you be happy if someone else took the same course of action as you did in this situation? And the *test of publicity* – would you be happy if your course of action was reported in the news? Does it stand up to public examination? (BACP, 2019). You should also work to the two key principles of *beneficence*, which is a commitment to the welfare of your participant and working towards the greater good, and *non-maleficence* which is about avoiding harming your participant.

You might like to read Case study 5.1, 'Whose voice?', in which Bethany found herself with a dilemma regarding who to listen to in a situation of interviewing an older woman in a residential care home. Bethany had to consider the ethics appropriate to those particular circumstances.

Case study 5.1

Whose voice?

Instructions: Read through the following real-life scenario and answer the questions below.

First visit

Upon arrival, the care home manager 'Trisha' gave Bethany a list of residents' names who she could approach to be interviewed. These were all people who the manager had judged to have the capacity to understand what an interview was about. As Bethany spoke to these selected residents, in the dining room, another resident, 'Daisy' (not selected by the manager) became curious and asked if she could take part in the research.

Two years previously, Daisy had taken part in another project that Bethany had worked on and Bethany had interviewed her for almost an hour. However, Daisy did not remember this previous research project.

Bethany asked Trisha if Daisy could be interviewed, to which she replied, 'No, she gets agitated and you wouldn't know from speaking to her that she does not have the mental capacity to take part'. A volunteer (and retired senior nurse) at the care home overheard this conversation and spoke to Bethany privately, out of earshot of the manager. She disagreed with Trisha and said she thought Daisy would be a good interviewee as she would offer a different perspective to the other residents.

Daisy was known for her strong views and critical opinions on the care she received, although she was generally happy in the home and there were no safeguarding concerns.

Second visit

One week later, Bethany returned to interview the other selected residents who had agreed to take part. The manager Trisha had unexpectedly left her job and there was a new acting manager (who was familiar with the residents after working for them for many years). The new manager said it was fine to interview Daisy, and Daisy was still excited to take part.

The ethical dilemma

The dilemma Bethany faced in this scenario was that Daisy may or may not have lacked the capacity to consent to be interviewed according to the Mental Health Act. The manager, Trisha may have been acting in Daisy's best interests in not allowing her to be interviewed. However, it may also have been true that the manager was being obstructive because Daisy was known for her strong opinions on the home.

Daisy appeared to understand the concept of research, had been interviewed on a previous occasion (although her mental capacity may have changed since then) and was requesting to take part. Should the manager have overruled this? Whose voice should Bethany have listened to?

What would you do?

- What would you have done if the original manager (Trisha) was still in the role?
- What would you do now that the manager has left and there is a new manager?
- What particular precautions would you take if you decided to interview Daisy?

Outcome

With the permission of the new manager and with Daisy's signed and verbal consent, the interview went ahead. Bethany was very mindful to watch for any apparent changes in Daisy's mental or physical health. She was particularly watching for signs of discomfort, agitation and forgetfulness. Bethany kept in mind that should those signs arise, she should gently bring the interview to an end, inform a member of staff, and the resulting interview data would not be used. In the end, Daisy remained happy and well throughout the interview, spoke lucidly and was able to remember events normally. The interview proceeded as normal and the data was used in the final report.

Table 5.2   Ethical scenarios

Read through the following situations based on real-life scenarios together as a group. Think about what the researcher should do next in this situation and what preventative or anticipatory measures (if any) could be taken to prevent the situation from arising			
	Scenario	What do you do next?	What could you have done to anticipate or prevent this situation? (If applicable)
1.	You are interviewing a participant in a café and you notice the place has gone quiet and the customers on the next table are listening in		
2.	You are interviewing a care home resident with a staff member present. The staff member appears a bit cheeky and constantly refers to the female resident as 'Grandma'. This makes you feel a bit uncomfortable		

(Continued)

Table 5.2 (Continued)

	Scenario	What do you do next?	What could you have done to anticipate or prevent this situation? (If applicable)
3.	In an interview, your participant appears to be upset by the memories the interview raises for him; he begins to cry		
4.	You are close to completing your project and realise you would like to archive the material with your institutional repository, but you have not asked for permission to share the interview transcripts		
5.	You are interviewing an 18-year-old drug-user about drug services in the area and how they can support him. He unexpectedly confesses to you that he was indirectly involved in an unsolved and serious criminal incident unrelated to the substance abuse that he is involved in		
6.	Your gatekeeper (the manager of a day centre for people with learning disabilities) gives you free rein over whomever you wish to interview at the day centre		

Top tip summary

- Ethics are an integral part of the entire research process and not a discrete stage.
- Ethics should be afforded serious attention and will usually pass through an ethical committee process before proceeding with research.
- There are a number of ethical frameworks which focus on the basic principles of avoiding harm, informed consent, the right to withdraw, maintaining data confidentiality and anonymity, and the clarity of independence of the research and its possible uses.
- The ethical frameworks exist to guide researchers and protect participants, rather than to be a hindrance to innovative research methodologies.
- The boundaries between ethical and unethical practices are not clear cut, and a sound and confident knowledge of ethical principles can allow for some flexibility in their application.

GET READY TO GO

---Learning objectives---

On completing this chapter, you should be able to:

- Identify appropriate research locations for conducting interviews
- Evaluate the best way to record the research encounter
- Recognise the importance of researcher safety
- Know what things to take with you to an interview.

This chapter offers an insight into the practicalities of getting ready to go into the interview encounter, including choosing the right location, considering researcher safety, checking and memorising (where possible) the interview guide, recording the encounter, and scheduling. We discuss the pros and cons of interviewing in public versus private spaces, or face to face or online, and what difference this can make to the data collected. We consider recording techniques, such as the use of dictaphones/voice recorders, mobile devices, note taking and memory. Finally, we show you how to keep a clear record of your participant contacts, which would include, for instance, basic biographical details and the length and location of the interview.

Where should I conduct my interviews?

The first thing to consider is where your interview will take place, and related to this your own safety, the safety of your participants and the quality of your data. Will you use a public place, a rented space, a workplace, an institution, your own home, or will you go to your interviewee's home? Will you be indoors or outdoors? Will you conduct the interviews in person or online? There are pros and cons to all of these arrangements, and each will have an effect on how your data is collected. Let's look at each of these locations in turn.

A public place

If you are interviewing someone co-presently (in person) whom you have never met before, a public place might be the most appropriate setting to ensure your own personal safety. Hopefully, there will be other people around should your interview encounter turn out to be a bit uncomfortable, and you have more opportunity to leave the space if you need to. Using a public place means you can create a neutral space, not influenced by power, which might come from interviewing someone in a private space. As you can see from Rob's story in Case study 6.1, the power dynamics of interviewing someone in their own home can have an interesting effect on the relationship.

The downside to interviewing in a public place is that you might face interruptions, background noise, a lack of privacy and poor quality audio recordings. When Bethany interviewed 'Karen', she originally agreed to meet in a large pub, but it was extremely busy, so she moved to a café above a theatre nearby. Bethany and Karen found a quiet spot, but halfway through the interview the theatre audience came out and the interview was disrupted for at least 15 minutes before they could start recording again. When Katy interviewed a participant in a café, she found that the recording was really difficult to transcribe and resulted in reliability errors in the transcription.

If recording outside, you might also need to consider the weather conditions and how they might affect both the quality of your interview recording and your and the participant's sense of comfort. Bethany once conducted interviews on some picnic benches outside a pub. This started as a nice location, on a sunny afternoon. However, the interview lasted a solid five hours (at the interviewee's request) and the benches quickly became an uncomfortable choice! You may also find that public places can be inhibiting for your participants, and they may not want to discuss personal issues or express deep emotions in public.

You might consider booking a room such as an office, a community hall or classroom, but this could have financial implications or be difficult to secure. Again, this would provide you with a neutral power space, but it could also be secluded and potentially threatening to a lone researcher, depending on who you are interviewing. If renting a space, always arrive early to check the place is open as expected, so you do not end up hanging around an unfamiliar place and then perhaps having to interview your participant in a less desirable location.

An online space

Interviewing people via an online platform, particularly during the COVID-19 pandemic, might mean that you are each situated within your own personal spaces at home. Under these circumstances, there is the potential for some of your personal effects and family interactions to be on show to your participant and for theirs to be on show to you. Perhaps you have to share your living space with housemates or family who hang around in the background of your call, or you might have to conduct your research interviews from your bedroom in order to get the best internet connection, or perhaps you have caring responsibilities and you are mindful about breaching their privacy whilst on a call to a participant. These can all pose dilemmas for your and your participant's privacy.

On Zoom, there is the option to create a virtual backdrop, but this is not always 100% effective if you have lots of clutter and do not have a green screen. One top tip is to hang a green blanket in your background and use that to enable the virtual background. You might want to extend that advice on how to hide a background to your participants too.

Seeing into the private world of our participant might be revealing for your research, in the same way as if you were to visit their home in person, but if the online interview is a matter of necessity (due to the pandemic) rather than through personal invitation then you might consider whether it is really ethical to observe their background activities. Think – would you want your background scrutinised by an interviewer without your permission?

However, this glimpse into each other's private world may also have an unexpected positive effect on the power dynamics and help build rapport. Small children interrupting, or showing off your pets, or talking about interesting background features such as a painting or other item, can create a humanising effect which can erode any perceived hierarchical differences. Indeed, Weller's (2017) young participants reported feeling more at ease when interviews were conducted online because some of the pressure and formality of the interview encounter was reduced and they were more used to engaging in an online space.

Your own home

Katy and I have personally never invited any participants to our home to be interviewed. We think this option should only be reserved for when you are interviewing people that you know *very* well, such as trusted family or close friends. Inviting strangers into your home to be interviewed has obvious security risks and blurs professional boundaries. It also creates a power imbalance in that you are automatically in a place of power over your participant. It might also be difficult to leave the encounter should things become awkward, as you would need to ask your participant to leave rather than politely making your excuses to leave someone else's home.

However, if this is a choice you make, then you should make your interviewee feel welcome. Offer them a drink or a small snack and find a clean and comfortable place for you both to sit. If you have pets, check with your participant whether they are comfortable with them being around or put the animal(s) in a separate room. Be clear about your time boundaries of how long the interview will last and stick to them, so that your interviewee is clear about when they will be expected to leave.

Your interviewee's home

Bethany has interviewed the majority of her participants in their own homes as she found it was an interesting source of additional contextual data and provided her with an incredibly rich picture of the lives of the people she studied. She was also conducting extremely sensitive and emotional interviews on topics which most participants would not be comfortable answering questions about in a public space. Katy has also conducted interviews in people's homes, mainly when interviewing about recycling practices or food preparation, so that the participants could demonstrate their practices at the same time as being interviewed. The majority of the experiences were extremely positive but there have also been some strange and slightly unnerving occurrences too. You might like to read Case studies 6.1 and 6.2 and discuss these in Activity 6.1.

Case study 6.1

A strange encounter at Rob's house

As I approached his front door, I noticed sweet wrappers and a pizza menu that had blown up to the front door with some old brown autumn leaves. The front garden was overgrown, but they all were in that street. I noticed, however, that amongst the over-grown look of the garden there were some pretty pink fuchsias. The front windows appeared quite dirty, perhaps mostly as a result of living near the main road. Rob didn't answer the door, so I was left wondering where he was. I stood alone in the street as it approached dusk. He arrived by car about five minutes later and let me in through the back door, perhaps explaining why the front door was so unkempt – he didn't use that entrance.

The house itself was quite extraordinary inside. The kitchen was decorated with bizarre ornaments and artwork, including a large pile of papier-mâché animals and a picture of a gnome. There were lots of pictures of a young girl with a big smile and children's artwork on the walls.

In the lounge, there was a wall mural of a beautiful lake and a tent. *Is this his attempt to escape to somewhere more exciting, to escape his problems?* I asked about the mural and whether he painted it and what made him decide to paint it. He replied, 'well, haven't you ever wanted to camp beside a beautiful lake? When I come home from work, I sit in my kitchen, put some music on and have a drink and suddenly I am beside this lake'.

The interview itself was extremely emotional, with Rob openly crying about the breakdown of his family.

At the end of the interview, when the recorder had been packed away and I was just about to get up to leave, he grabbed a nearby flexi-necked desk lamp which was turned on, turning it into my face and saying, 'right, the spotlight is on you now'. He then proceeded to be quite forceful in his mannerisms and spoke unflatteringly about the person who had referred him to me to be interviewed (even though Rob had willingly agreed to be interviewed and had signed consent forms). It was at this point that I realised that I had not told anyone where I was going, and I did not have a mobile phone with me.

Bethany's reflection

This was a strange moment at Rob's house, and it was a turning point in my research practice. In this situation, I became acutely aware that emotional distress which was brought up in a highly sensitive interview could be acted out in unexpected ways. In future interviews, I made sure that participants were very well informed about the kinds of things they might talk about (although Rob also had a detailed information sheet and consent form and was happy to talk). I also made sure that I took a mobile phone and a charger with me. I now always let a trusted contact know the name and address of where I am going, when I am leaving and when to expect my return.

Case study 6.2

Space as a source of data – Fay's house

I arrived at Fay's house and knocked on her door four times before she came to it and called out, 'Who is it?' I said, 'It's Bethany'. She replied 'Bethany? I don't know a Bethany'. I continued, 'I have come to do the interview you agreed to'. She then flung open the door, dressed only in a small dressing gown, and shouted 'Oh, bloody hell. I forgot about that. Excuse the mess and I will have to go upstairs and get dressed. Sit down if you can find a space. You will have to excuse the state of me. I went out last night to see a show and got pissed. I normally work nights and

(Continued)

that was why I was in bed'. She had an ironing board in front of an old fireplace and small TV. There was no carpet on the floor and the walls were bare, with newly plastered areas. Her handbag contents were spilt all over the floor and furniture as if she had thrown her bag across the room. Cash, makeup, keys, cards and so on were scattered far and wide across the place.

There was only one seat in the room, which was covered by a throw and had piles of washing all over it. I tried to move some of the things so I could sit down, and she perched on the arm of the chair. It was not the ideal set-up and neither of us was comfortable. Soon after we began the interview, we were interrupted by a man wanting to come and fix her boiler, who then knocked loudly in the kitchen. Fay said, 'Let's go to my friend's house instead. I have a key to let myself in'. So, we packed up and went up the road to her neighbour's house. They were not in, so Fay used her spare key to let us in, uninvited, which I was a bit uncomfortable with.

Bethany's reflection

Fay's life story interview was structured in a very chaotic fashion, which I felt reflected the chaos and confusion she felt from her past and in her current life. At one point of particular distress, she changed the subject quickly and continuously. Fay had few qualms about opening up to me and I felt she was using me as a therapeutic means of unloading her problems. The interview can be a cathartic opportunity and can even be empowering to some people who previously might not have had the opportunity to express themselves. She even said to me at one point, 'it's great to tell this actually'. Prior to the interview, she said she would 'like to be psychoanalysed'; and throughout the interview, she expressed her need for counselling. During the interview, I often saw Fay, eyes closed, lost in her vividly recalled descriptions. I often felt as if I was like an analyst and she oscillated between getting lost in her past and experiencing a rising panic as she returned to her present situation. She was extremely open, and I was frequently surprised at her candid honesty. Her narrative often came across as unrestrained and sometimes uncontrolled, which are characteristics she recognises and dislikes in her own personality. I felt her home environment was very much an outer reflection of her inner world.

Activity 6.1

Discussing the case studies

Read through the case studies for Rob and Fay which were derived from Bethany's field notes, taken after the respective interviews, and discuss the questions below.

- How might we interpret the behaviour of Rob and Fay?
- What might all of these clues in their homes tell us about them as people?

- To what extent is it important to be observant of a participant's behaviour in an interview?
- To what extent is it important to be observant of the space in which you interview someone?
- What personal risk did Bethany put herself in when conducting these interviews?

Things to consider before the interview

A day or so before meeting your interviewee, it is good practice to contact your participant to remind them about the interview, so that you save any embarrassment if you turn up unexpectedly, and also to save yourself time and resources on a wasted journey. The same applies to online interviews. It is useful to send a calendar invite so your participant has the date saved.

Set out for your journey to the interview leaving plenty of time and extra time for contingencies, such as traffic jams or delays in public transport, or getting lost! It is better to get there early, compose yourself and refresh your memory of your interview guide than to arrive flustered, panicked, apologetic and sweaty. If conducting your interviews online, check that your links work in advance, that you have stable internet, and join the video call at least five or ten minutes before to adjust the settings and get comfortable.

What do I need to take with me?

There are a few essential items which you will need to take with you to any interview. We have created these toolkits for you to tick off the items as you prepare for your interviews.

Box 6.1 ───────────────────────────────────────

Toolkits

Face-to-face interviewing toolkit

- Consent form
- Information sheet
- Interview guide (your set of questions)

(Continued)

- Contact details of your participant (name, address and phone number)
- Research diary/journal
- Plain paper/notebook
- Spare batteries for your audio recorder
- Pen
- Digital recorder
- Mobile phone
- Mobile phone charger
- Tissues
- Bottle of water
- Details of public transport routes or local taxi firms
- Change for parking or transport fares.

Online interview toolkit

- A fully charged laptop, or desktop computer, with good internet connection
- Consent form and information sheet – emailed in advance
- Interview guide
- Email address and phone number for your participant
- Plain paper/notebook
- Pen
- Drink of water
- Tissues.

Interview nerves

It is likely that you will be feeling quite nervous about conducting interviews. Even experienced interviewers can feel anxious – for Katy, it is often at the start of a project when the guide is still new or when meeting interviewees who are very accomplished in their field that the nerves kick in. It is perfectly normal to feel nervous as conducting an interview does involve putting into practice a range of skills and managing the encounter with confidence. See Box 6.2 for our top tips on dealing with interview nerves.

Many students do not anticipate beforehand that this might be a nerve-wracking event and these nerves can then affect the interview – for example, you may forget to ask open questions or rush through the encounter. Although you may feel nervous, you should not forget that your interviewee may also be feeling quite anxious and will be looking to you to guide them through the process. However, some interviewees – particularly experts or elites – will be very used to being interviewed and will therefore be curious about who you are and what you want from them. We cover the elite/expert interview in Chapter 9.

Box 6.2

Top tips for dealing with interview nerves

- *Be well prepared* – e.g. know your interview guide, have a few practice interviews under your belt, make sure your interview bag is packed, plan the route to your interview location and be sure to leave in plenty of time. Be in control of the things you can be
- *Think of some neutral topics* that you can discuss before the interview starts to put the interviewee at ease, such as the weather, pets, a recent movie
- *Have an introduction to your research ready* and rehearsed. Do not assume that just because you sent the information via email or letter that your interviewees have read this
- *Take deep breaths and remind yourself that your interviewee is human too* and is not expecting a robot to interview them. It is OK to display some nerves. But it can help to remember that this interview is not a life/death scenario and probably the worst thing that could happen is that the interview data is not as good as you had hoped for. Even if the interview goes badly, you can learn from the experience and will become a better interviewer for it
- *Be aware of how you normally respond when you are nervous* – ask yourself, are you likely to talk too quickly, blush, forget what you are saying, try to remove yourself from the situation? Are there any strategies you could employ to minimise these responses? For example, both of us are aware that we can blush when we are nervous, particularly on our neck and chest, so we often wear a scarf or high-necked top to disguise this.

Arriving at your interview

In a face-to-face interview, upon arrival you should greet your interviewee, perhaps with a handshake or a warm greeting (as long as there are no social distancing measures in place). Be careful not to go in for a hug unless they instigate that first – not everyone is comfortable with hugging and such close contact. Take your cue from your participant.

Keep your greeting friendly but professional. It is courteous to ask your participant how they would like to be addressed and to not assume they shorten their name. Bethany would be annoyed if someone assumed her name was 'Beth' and Katy prefers to be known by the shortened version of her full name 'Kathryn'. You might want to address your participant by their title and surname: 'Mrs Smith', 'Mr Jones', 'Dr Ahmed', and unless they correct you to use their first name, continue with the formalities.

Those first few moments are crucial for setting the tone of the interview to follow. You want to appear in control of the situation and as the 'host' for the experience to follow, even if you are not on 'home ground' (Yeo et al., 2014: 186). You should take charge by explaining what is about to happen, engaging in friendly small talk, and checking with your participant that they are comfortable to continue. If you are conducting the interview in someone's home or office, your interviewee will probably offer you a drink as a mark of hospitality. It is a good idea to accept this hospitality as sharing a drink together will help make the encounter feel more sociable. If you are holding the interview in a café or public place, offer to buy your participant a cup of tea/coffee for the same reason.

It is important to build trust and rapport and to break any barriers down when you arrive. You can do this by engaging in some small talk as you enter the space. You might consider talking about the weather or their family. If interviewing in someone's home, look around for clues as to what their hobbies are. You might create small talk over things like an interesting ornament, artwork on the walls, their lovely garden, or their pets. Avoid talking about political or sensitive matters which could create tensions before you have even begun the interview. The more relaxed an interviewee is, the more they will be able to offer you in-depth and reflective responses. This applies to both co-present interviews and interviews online, although we have found that there is less space for 'small talk' in the online setting. Weller (2017) reflects that the greetings at the start of an online interview can limit opportunities for building rapport because more attention is placed on dealing with connectivity and technical issues.

Setting the scene

Once you are in your interview setting, you may want to arrange your space, so it is more conducive to conducting an interview. If interviewing in someone's home, you might politely ask for a TV or radio to be turned down, or a washing machine to be turned off. You might want to ask for a more private space if there are other people around who might interrupt or listen in to the discussion. This is particularly important when interviewing online.

You should position the audio recorder between you and your interviewee and test that it is picking up both of your voices clearly. If there is a discrepancy between the quality and clarity of the audio recording between your voice and that of your interviewee, place the recorder so that it picks up your participant's voice more than it does yours. It is more important to capture their data than your own voice. You will also likely be able to recall the questions you asked even if you cannot hear them so clearly. Make sure that both you and your participant are seated comfortably as you could potentially be sat in that position for a couple of hours. Online, you should remember to press record!

Once comfortable, you should offer a brief summary of what the interview will be about, go over the consent form and information sheet again with them, even if it has been signed in advance, and remind them about being recorded.

Box 6.3

Stop & Reflect

What would you do?

Table 6.1 details a series of difficult situations that both of us have encountered when arriving at an interview. Take a few moments to either discuss with a classmate, or jot down your thoughts about how you would react to these situations. You will see in the table some of the things that we did and things we could have done.

Table 6.1 Handling difficult situations at the beginning of an interview

Scenario	What did we do?
You arrive at the office of an important interviewee, having arranged the interview about a month previously. Your interviewee has forgotten he had an appointment with you	Katy asked whether it was still possible to have the interview now or at another time, and fortunately the interviewee was free for 45 minutes to conduct the interview. Had he not been free for long enough, she would have rearranged the interview To prevent this situation from arising, it would have been a good idea to email or call the interviewee a few days before the scheduled interview to confirm the appointment
You arrive for the interview and ask your interviewee about her new baby, to help establish rapport. She then spends the next half an hour telling you about her children	When this happened to Katy, she chose to let her interviewee confide in her and listened attentively. She recognised that a new mum might be craving some adult company and she felt that this was a good way to create a friendly atmosphere before the interview commenced. Feminist models of interviewing stress the importance of two-way exchange, rather than the interviewer dominating the encounter. Katy did check the interviewee was free for the whole morning about 15 minutes in and as Katy hadn't got any other interviews booked for the day, she had the time to spare How you handle this situation will depend on several things – do you and the interviewee still have time to conduct the interview after this initial chat (another good reason not to book too many interviews on one day); might what she says be relevant to your project (although this would not be interview data per se, you might make some notes about the discussion in your journal to help you when you come to analyse your data); she may be talking about her baby because she doesn't want to do the interview (although this is unlikely in this situation, it might be the case when interviewing on sensitive topics)
You are offered a cup of tea when you arrive at your participant's home, but you don't like tea	Bethany does not like any hot drinks but accepting a drink is an important marker of hospitality in British households (and offices). To refuse is to refuse the chance of intimacy that sharing a drink can offer. It can also appear rude to not share a drink with your interviewee. Chatting over a tea or coffee acts as an important icebreaker and can help to establish rapport between yourself and your interviewee. Bethany tends to ask for a glass of water, so that she is still accepting her interviewee's hospitality

(Continued)

Table 6.1 (Continued)

Scenario	What did we do?
Your participant has a time lag and their video is freezing, making it very difficult for you to communicate with them	Connection problems are one of the recurrent issues with online interviews. In this situation, you should ask your participant to try logging off and then back in again. You may find a different device is more reliable than another so if they have a phone, they could connect to the interview this way rather than via their main computer. Sometimes muting yourself or turning off the video makes the connection clearer, but this will have implications for the interaction going forward. We would recommend trying the other steps first before you resort to cameras off, which would make the interview more like a telephone encounter. You may consider rescheduling if you think the problem is caused by poor weather conditions
Your interviewee refuses to sign the consent form at the beginning of the interview	Katy has found that expert or elite interviewees will often refuse to sign the consent form at the beginning of the interview. This is usually because these individuals are speaking on behalf of their organisation and they do not want to consent to their words being used before they know what the questions are and what they have said. The way Katy handles this is to introduce the consent form at the beginning of each interview so that any questions can be raised, and it is clear to participants how the data will be used (do not assume that just because you have sent the forms in advance, they will have been read). But she then says, 'you don't have to sign this now if you are uncomfortable doing so before the interview; we can return to the form at the end of the interview once you know what you have said, if you prefer'. This deals with some of the suspicions that interviewees might have about interviewers trying to catch them out, and makes consent a more negotiated process
Your interviewee does not want to have their interview audio-recorded	This has happened only once to Bethany but has never happened to Katy. Most participants are happy to be recorded and are aware of this when agreeing to the interview (it should be in your letter to your participant and in the information sheet). For Bethany, the refusal to be recorded occurred during a project on drug use amongst homeless people, and the tape recorder was viewed with suspicion. In this situation, the interviewer must make notes during the interview and type these up immediately after the interview. If your interviews involve illegal or very sensitive information, you should be prepared for this possibility We stress that it is quite rare for people to refuse to be recorded, however what can often happen is that once the tape recorder has been turned off, our participants will tell us things they did not want on tape. We have to respect their wish for this data not to be recorded, but as with the case of the talkative participant, you might be able to record some of the details in your reflexive journal and return to them when you are analysing your interviews (see Chapter 11)

Keeping safe

Keeping safe whilst travelling to an interview destination

You should always think about your personal safety when interviewing, particularly interviewing strangers in their own home. Travelling to and from your destination should also be planned carefully.

When travelling to your interview destination, you need to consider the best routes and transport options for both directions of the journey. Think, if you are travelling to your destination by public transport, will that same transport be available for a return journey? Make sure you take note of which train or bus you need to catch, what the timetable is for that route, and where the nearest stop is to your destination. Bethany once finished an interview late in London only to find that the trains had stopped running in the early evening from her closest tube stop. Make sure you have money available to travel by taxi in an emergency, but again research reliable and genuine taxi firms in that area in advance of your interview. Do not just jump into the first cab you see. Try to avoid walking alone at night or in the dark and stick to well-lit areas, and where possible avoid underpasses and alleyways.

Keeping safe online

Your safety is just as important online. When conducting interviews with strangers online, it is good practice to set a password for entry to the interview. Also, set some boundaries at the start of the interview around your expectations, such as the use of bad language, using their mobile phone during the interview, making sure they switch off their camera and audio if they leave it unattended, even for a short while; and if the person behaves inappropriately on camera towards you, make your excuses and terminate the call.

Recording the interview

Should you record the interview? If so, how? This depends on whether your interviewee gives consent for you to record it. Sometimes interviewees are nervous about the presence of a recording device. As researchers, we often hear participants say, 'I hate the sound of my own voice'. But, as researchers, we do not always like to hear our own voice either! It is quite unusual for a participant to completely refuse to be audio-recorded. With some reassurance about how the recording will be used, most interviewees will agree. We usually state to them that the recording is for our own records and that only me and perhaps a transcriber will actually hear the recording. We also tell participants that it is helpful for us to record them in order to gain an accurate account of their interview. If a participant absolutely refuses to be recorded, they may be happy for you to take written notes.

There are many digital recorders on the market at the moment and they are relatively inexpensive. Investing in one of these is a good idea as the quality of the recording is usually very good. You must learn how to use the device in advance of meeting your participant though, as careless use of such a device could result in accidentally deleting a recording. It is advisable to do a test recording with your participant to check the quality of the sound before going ahead with the interview.

Sometimes exterior noises or echoes in the interview environment can adversely affect your recording and can make it difficult to transcribe. If you have a recording that is difficult to hear, you might look at audio tools to help optimise the audio quality, such as Audacity, Ocenaudio or WavePad.

You can use your phone as a recorder; however, we would caution against this for two key reasons. First, phone batteries can drain rapidly if they are using certain apps and you may rely on your phone to keep safe on your journey home and to let your base contact know the interview has finished. Second, a recording may take up a lot of memory on your phone and you may not be able to save it properly. We recommend recording on two devices – a digital voice recorder and a tablet, or two digital recorders. This means that if one device is not recording correctly then you have a backup recording. When saving the recording to the device, make sure it has a clear file name so you can retrieve it at a later date. Finally, always remember to create backups of your recording as soon as you can.

If you are conducting interviews using video-conferencing software such as Microsoft Teams, Zoom or Google Meet, there is an option in the settings to record the interview. It is, of course, really important to inform your participant before you start recording. If you are using Zoom, the audio from a Zoom meeting is automatically transcribed and will appear as a separate VTT file in the list of your recorded meetings. It is important to listen to your recording again, though, to more accurately capture the words or add in punctuation which might have been missed in the transcription.

Box 6.4

Top tip

Record your immediate impressions and observations about the interview, by talking into your voice recorder on your way home. Then later transcribe this recording to include as part of your field notes.

Table 6.2 Example of participant record-keeping sheet

Int. No.	Pseudonym	Age	Marital Status	Children	Interviewee's Level of Education	Interviewee's Occupation	Place of Interview	Date of Interview	Time of Interview
1	Jack	42	Married	Twin girls, aged 7, who live at home	MA	Academic researcher	His work – booked an empty office	01/05/2019	1–3pm
2	Rob	50	Divorced	Three children: two boys (18, at uni, and 16, lives with mother) and one girl (6, lives with mother)	BSc	Self-employed computer technician	His home	02/06/2019	2.00–4.30pm
3	Kathleen	46	Married	Two children, a girl (16) and a boy (14), both living at home	O levels	Beauty therapist	Her home	17/07/2019	1.00–4.15pm
4	Lisa	45	Married	Two children, a boy (24) and a girl (19); both left home for uni, but both have returned	O levels and hairdressing NVQ	Part-time home hairdresser	Her home	20/07/2019	12.30–3.30pm
5	Janet	40	Married	Three boys, aged 16, 14 and 9, all living at home	MA	Stay-at-home mum	Her home	04/08/2019	10.30–12.45pm

Keeping track of interviewees

You may find yourself interviewing many participants, sometimes within a short time frame. It is therefore important to keep a good record of your participants, when you have interviewed them, and their biographical details. This will help you to identify any gaps in your sampling and will be a significant aid in your analysis and writing-up stages. See Table 6.2 for an example of how you might record participant information. You could add other columns which give specific details relevant to your research sample too, such as 'race', class and sexuality.

Top tip summary

- Think about the pros and cons of your interview environment.
- If interviewing someone in their own home, be aware of your personal safety.
- Set clear boundaries and expectations with your participant when interviewing online.
- Always take care when travelling to and from your interview destination.
- Use a digital recorder to record your interview or use the record function on your online platform.
- Back up your recording as soon as possible or download your audio recording from the cloud.
- Use the toolkit checklists (Box 6.1) to ensure you have everything you need with you.
- Keep a detailed log of your interviews.

CREATE YOUR DATA

Learning objectives

On completing this chapter, you should be able to:

- Recognise the importance of developing trust and rapport with a research participant
- Understand the role of the interviewer at different stages of an interview
- Apply key qualitative interviewing skills
- Practise the art of active listening.

Now we have reached the crucial point in the interview process that many of you will have bought (or borrowed) this book for – the point at which you create your data through the interview encounter. The steps that preceded this stage were crucial to get you to this point and they should not be rushed or skipped. This chapter deals with the key skills and qualities needed when undertaking a qualitative interview; starting from the point of meeting with your participant and moving from this initial encounter to a situation where the participant is sharing their insights with you. We discuss the key stages that most interviews pass through and then go on to think about the key skills needed to manage interview flow, including using your interview guide flexibly, asking follow-up questions, the use of silence and active listening.

In this chapter, you will learn how to ask questions which probe and encourage participants. There are activities for you to complete throughout the chapter to help prepare you for an interview encounter, for example on probing participants for more details, and on practising active listening. However, our biggest piece of practical advice is to conduct several pilot interviews and interrogate your performance as an interviewer. This was suggested in Chapter 3 when developing your interview guide, and we repeat its importance again here. The best way to learn how to do qualitative interviews is to practise them and to thoroughly reflect on the experience.

Key interview skills

The success of a qualitative interview depends to a large part on the skills of the interviewer. The interview encounter involves putting these skills into practice all at once to enable your participant to feel at ease to talk freely about the topic of interest. Building a rapport with your participant is crucial and can be achieved through creating an initial friendly atmosphere at the opening stage of the interview, and maintained by really listening to what your participant says and valuing their contribution to the project.

Box 7.1

Stop & Reflect

What key skills or qualities do you think a qualitative interviewer needs to have?

Take a moment to jot down as many as you can. The list below outlines some of the key skills we thought of, but you can add to this:

- **Curiosity**: 'If what people have to say about their world is generally boring to you, then you will never be a great interviewer. Unless you are fascinated by the rich variation in human experience, qualitative interviewing will become drudgery' (Patton, 2002: 341)
- **Patience**: You may have to try more than once to get your participant to talk freely about your topic. It may be, for example, that you need to offer a listening ear to a new mum or an expert who is talking in detail about something they are proud of before you can get to the topic you want discussed
- **Composure**: Although you may be feeling nervous about interviewing or anxious about something your participant has said, presenting a calm exterior is a key skill to develop. Appearing composed will best support your participant to engage with the interview – however, it's a good idea to think

about how you might deal with a situation that you would want to remove yourself from, such as if you are feeling very uncomfortable or at risk

- **Attentive listening and concentration**: Really listening to what your participant says and being able to link this back to your interview goals will enable you to ask relevant follow-up questions and gather high-quality data. Listening is one of the best ways you can respect your participant
- **Good memory**: Remembering what your participant has told you earlier in the interview is important for coming up with appropriate follow-up questions and for spotting when similarities and inconsistencies occur in people's narratives
- **Flexibility and quick thinking**: A good interviewer should be able to adapt their approach in response to the interviewee they have in front of them. This might mean covering a later part of the guide sooner than anticipated or thinking on your feet to re-word interview questions as you go
- **Empathy**: A good interviewer will respect their participant's viewpoint, allowing them to tell their story on their own terms, and will aim to understand their position rather than judge them.

Stages of the interview

You have secured the interview, know your guide inside out and arrive at the agreed meeting place in plenty of time, with your interview bag packed. Now for the important first moments of the interview where you and your interviewee meet for the first time and establish the interview relationship. Most interviews follow a relatively predictable pattern, moving from easy and non-threatening open questions through to more challenging and in-depth questions before the interview winds down. You thought about the flow of the interview when you were developing your guide. In Chapter 3, we said that there are four key types of question: the introductory or opening question, main questions, follow-up questions (sometimes called probes and prompts) and closing questions/remarks (see Table 3.3). These elements make up the key stages of the interview (see Table 7.1).

The interviewer has a different role to play at each of these stages, and we'll briefly outline some important features of each of these stages below.

In the **introductory** phase, you introduce yourself and informally chat with your participant, trying to connect on a personal level. It is useful to have a few neutral topics ready to discuss – perhaps talking about their pets or a piece of artwork in their room. The aim here is build an initial rapport and create a relaxed atmosphere. If you are conducting the interview online, the first moments of the interview will be taken up with checking the connection is stable and that your interviewee has a quiet space to talk, free from distractions. You should introduce

Table 7.1 The key stages of an interview

Interview stage	Types of question	Interviewer's role during this stage
Introduction	Interviewee's questions should be answered	• Establish initial rapport • Check connection and sort any technical issues (if online) • Introduce research • Obtain informed consent • Remind interviewee you want to hear about their experiences in their own words
Warm-up	Opening questions	• Put participant at ease • Find out basic biographical details • Help participants to give full and detailed answers
Main body	Main questions, follow-up questions	• Guide participant through the key themes of the interview • Listen attentively • Probe for depth, breadth and clarity • Encourage the participant • Avoid judgement • Observe body language • Talk less than the interviewee • Keep an eye on the clock
Winding down	Closing questions	• Signal that the encounter will end soon • Encourage the participant to reflect on the interview • End on a positive note
Conclusion	Interviewee's questions should be answered	• Thank participant for their time • Reiterate the next steps and what they can expect from you • Listen out for 'doorstep data'

your research and explain what the interviewee can expect from the process. This is where the participant information sheet and consent form (see Chapter 5) are discussed. It is good practice to send copies of these before the interview, though you should expect to go through them at this point because not everyone will have read them closely. Your interviewee should have the opportunity to ask questions. You must also legally check that they are happy for the interview to be recorded. If you will be dealing with very sensitive topics, you might want to flag this up and remind participants that they do not have to answer any question they are uncomfortable with. Finally, it is a good idea to highlight that the interview is not a survey where yes/no answers are expected. By telling them you want to hear about their experiences in their own words, you are also reminding your participant of how much you value their expertise.

The **warm-up** phase should put your participant at ease. We recommended in Chapter 3 that a 'Tell me about yourself' type question often works well here. This gives the interviewer the opportunity to learn useful demographic details, at the same time as the interviewee answers a low-stake but hopefully easy question. This is the ideal time to model the sort of interaction you are looking for in the interview. So, if you receive a one-word or one-sentence answer, you should encourage your participant to give fuller answers, using probes (see below). You are setting the tone of the interview that will follow in this warm-up phase, so care should be taken to elicit in-depth and rich responses. In the extract Katy shares in Box 7.3, you'll see how failing to do this led to a poor qualitative interview.

In the **main body** of the interview, you are putting into practice a wide range of qualitative interviewing skills to cover the key themes and topics on your interview guide. You should be listening carefully to what your participant says and probing, where appropriate, for more depth and detail. You will be working extremely hard in this phase to keep the interview on track, both in terms of topics covered and the time you have. But also, you must respect the interviewee in front of you to gather their unique account.

In the **winding down** phase, you are signalling to the interviewee that the encounter will shortly close. Don't end the interview too abruptly, especially if it has been emotional for your participant. You can signal this phase by saying, 'Coming to the last question now' or by giving them the opportunity to reflect on the interview so far, for instance 'Given what we have spoken about today, how do you feel about X?' It is also a good idea to ask participants if there is anything they wanted to talk about but haven't yet done so. Generally, interviewees will cover the topics important to them, even if you haven't directly asked. However, it might be that your interviewee has not had the opportunity to introduce an important topic. So, use the winding down phase to check this. You do not want to finish the interview without being sure your participant feels they have talked about everything that matters to them in relation to your topic.

Finally, in the **concluding** phase, you should thank your participant for being interviewed and remind them what will happen next. Be realistic about what you promise at the end of an interview. It can be tempting to over-promise at this point because you are so grateful to your participant, but not meeting these expectations will damage the relationship with your participant going forward. For example, if you plan to send copies of the interview transcript or a summary of your key findings, explain to your participant how long these things will take to prepare. If the consent form was not signed in the introductory phase, now is the time to return to the form and negotiate the terms on which you can use the information. The concluding phase is also marked by switching off the recording equipment.

You might find that without the recorder running, your participant suddenly becomes talkative about something they were reluctant to say 'on the record'. Yeo et al. (2014) refer to this as 'doorstep data'. With consent procedures in mind, think carefully about how, or even if, you can use this data.

Managing interview flow

How an interview moves through the phases above will depend on the ways you, the interviewer, manage this encounter. An interviewer who only asks the questions on their guide and misses opportunities to encourage their participant to elaborate and clarify, will find the interview encounter stilted and brief. Meanwhile, the interviewer who actively listens and probes for more detail will likely walk away from the encounter feeling they have collected useful and rich data. Your approach to interviewing should be 'responsive' to the participant in front of you, to borrow from Rubin and Rubin (2012). Below are some key tips for achieving a responsive approach to interviewing.

Managing your guide

Because you spent a lot of time thinking about your questions when developing your guide (see Chapter 3), you have already laid the groundwork for the interview. You should know your guide inside-out, so you are in the best position to use it flexibly. It can be disconcerting for a participant if you are constantly breaking eye contact to look at your guide to check the next question. Reading from a schedule can make you look unprepared and sound a little stilted and robotic, rather than naturally flowing. If you are looking at your guide, you might also be tempted not to listen as closely because you will be scanning the guide for the next question. Take your interview guide with you so you can glance at it if you get really stuck, though both Katy and Bethany tend to put the guide to one side and only check it discretely.

Guides are there as a safety net and to help you make sure you cover everything that is important for your project. They should be adapted and developed with each interviewee. For example, your participant may start talking about something later in your guide towards the beginning of their interview. You will need to make an on-the-spot decision about whether to probe around their response immediately or wait until later in the interview. If you choose to follow up on it later, make a few quick notes to yourself and be careful to acknowledge that you are returning to a point they have already made. Nothing damages rapport more than if your participant thinks you aren't listening to them.

Activity 7.1

Taking notes in an interview

It is often a good idea to have a piece of paper and pen handy when you are conducting an interview. Jotting down the odd word whilst your participant is talking can serve as a good reminder of something that needs to be followed up on later. However, you should not be writing long notes to yourself or breaking eye contact with your interviewee for too long as this is distracting. Practise taking notes without looking at the paper in front of you. The next time you attend a lecture or sit down with a friend, experiment with this type of note-taking.

Don't feel you have to ask every question on your guide if your participant has addressed it already or if you think it no longer relevant. If you are pressed for time, be clear with yourself about how long you want to spend on each key theme in your guide, and be sure to pace the discussion and move on to new themes to cover everything you want to. You can use phrases like 'Moving on to the next question now' or 'That's interesting and links to the next point I want to ask about'.

You will constantly be judging whether to allow your participant to digress and follow up on new leads. It can be difficult in the moment to determine whether what someone is telling you is relevant. If you cut someone off too early, you may miss important information. But if you leave them to talk at length about something that turns out not to be relevant, you will lose precious interview time. It is a challenge. You need to weigh up how much time you both have for the interview and the key principles of the approach to interviewing that you are taking – a more open approach would allow for more digression than a semi-structured one.

Asking follow-up questions

With a responsive approach to interviewing, it is important to move beyond the questions on your guide and ask questions that relate to what your participant is telling you. Questions developed in the moment of the interview are usually referred to as probes or prompts. We mentioned these in Chapter 3. As a reminder, **probes** are 'questions, comments, or gestures used by the interviewer to help manage the conversation' (Rubin and Rubin, 2012: 118). They are probably the most important tool an interviewer employs to help participants to elaborate on their answers and to clarify/confirm that the interviewer has understood what they are told. Although we have labelled this section as 'questions', many probes are non-verbal (such as silence and expectant body language).

Prompts, on the other hand, are issues explicitly raised by the researcher 'rather than issues raised by the interviewee' (Yeo et al., 2014: 196). Prompts may be included on your guide but will only be asked if your interviewee does not raise them on their own. We would recommend that prompts are included as keywords on your guide as a reminder, rather than as fully worded questions. In general, it is better to probe around an answer from your participant rather than prompt them. However, there will be some occasions where you have no choice but to prompt if you want them to address a specific issue.

Formulating good follow-up questions and probes is one of the key skills of an effective qualitative interviewer. It is something that takes a lot of practice and requires you to listen very carefully to what your participant is telling you. There are several activities at the end of this section that will help develop your active listening skills. For now, we focus on the sorts of probes and follow-ups that you might use to encourage your participants to give you more depth and detail.

There are different types of probe at your disposal (see Table 7.2 and Boxes 7.2 and 7.3), which have different functions depending on what information you want to gather. It is important to mix up the types of probe you use and not to over-rely on one type. Novice interviewers will often over-use the 'why' question, but this is not a great probe because it tends to result in 'overreflected intellectualized' responses (Brinkmann and Kvale, 2015: 159). It is better to get your participant to talk through concrete examples of things that have happened to them and how they felt about them. Also, as you will see in the next chapter, some experiences are beyond words and a 'why' question will be unable to capture this. The odd 'why' question is fine but using it repeatedly is poor practice.

A good place to probe is usually when a participant assumes you know what they mean. An interviewee might say, 'Oh, you know what those young people are like round here'. Perhaps you do, but you want to hear that from your participant, so you could follow this with an elaboration probe like, 'Could you say more about what the young people are like around here?' This is a particular problem if you are interviewing someone you know well as you will have a shared context that can make it difficult to probe effectively.

Table 7.2 Types of interview probe

Type of probe	Examples
Non-verbal probes: using simple body language and silence are gentle probes that can signal to your participant you want to hear more from them	• Silence (see below) • Nodding • Sitting upright and slightly forward with arms open (rather than lounging back with arms crossed)

Type of probe	Examples
Encouragement probes: use these when you want to reassure your participant that what they are telling you is relevant, and you want to hear more from them	• Repeating something the participant has said as a question (see Box 7.2) • 'Mmm' or 'I see' (but use them sparingly as they can quickly become annoying or close down discussion) • Tell me more
Elaboration probes: use these when participants tell you something and you want more details from them. They may tell you a story but only do so superficially or use a phrase like 'you know what I mean'. Never assume you know what they mean (even if you think you do); use elaboration probes to encourage them to provide more information and depth	• Can you say a bit more about that? • Could you give an example? (such as Katy asking what is a high-level chore, Box 7.3) • Can you tell me exactly what happened? • How did you respond when that happened? • Why was that? (but avoid over-using why) • Then what? • How so? • What makes you say that? • Listen for adjectives and ask what made them describe something this way, e.g. 'what made the walk really relaxing?' or 'in what ways was it difficult?'
Clarification probes: use these when you want to check your understanding of what the participant has said (see Box 7.2)	• Can you run that by me again, please? • Sorry this may be obvious, but can I check what you meant when you said… • What do you mean by 'X'?
Steering probes: use these when you want to get your interviewee back on track, or if you want to remind them of something they have already said	• Could we go back to something you said earlier about 'X'? • That's interesting and links to my next question • Earlier you said 'X'; can we revisit this as there is a question I wanted to ask • I'm conscious of time; do you mind if we move to the next question?

Box 7.2

Examples of encouragement and clarification probes

Encouragement probe – in the following dialogue, notice how Bethany repeats Katherine's words to encourage her to continue:

Bethany: Yes. Do you feel that your relationship has changed with your daughter since you've moved here?

Katherine: Yes. Bound to.

(Continued)

Bethany: It's bound to.
Katherine: Mmm.
Bethany: Yes. In what ways do you think it has changed?
Katherine: Erm, well, the, um, the balance has changed, hasn't it? Now, she's doing me the favours, you know. Mmm.

Clarification probe – in this example, Bethany thinks she knows what Rodney means but he has used a term that has a different meaning, so Bethany checks her understanding:

Bethany: Have you noticed any kind of physical changes in your body since turning 40?
Rodney: In my body ... yes. Mmmm ... how can I put it ... getting more ... how can I put it ... sex ... sex appeal, you know what I mean ... well ...
Bethany: Sex appeal or sex drive?
Rodney: Sex drive you know what I mean. I find I'm harder now than what I've ever been so ... yep, and it's good for the wife as well.

All interviewers have had interviews that go less well than hoped for and it is a good idea to look back at the follow-up questions you asked to see if there is something you can learn from your approach. In Box 7.3, Katy provides examples of good and poor follow-up questions and reflects on what went well and badly.

Box 7.3

Examples of good and poor follow-up questions

Good follow-up – notice how I asked Paula to elaborate on how she understands the work associated with recycling by probing her to explain her classification of a low-level chore. This simple probe elicited in-depth insights from Paula:

Paula: The recycling is a chore yeah, but it's not very onerous, it's just a low-level chore I'd call it, so manageable but could be made a bit easier, but it's fine.
Katy: What would be a high-level chore?
Paula: A high-level chore? [laughs] Well, erm ... well I suppose I meant low-level in the sense that it doesn't take a lot of time, I'll have to think about what a high-level chore would be ... well I would put cleaning above that and although I have someone who comes to do the cleaning every 2 weeks, I would call that a medium-level chore because there's actually a lot to do and it involves equipment like Hoovers and stuff so it's not, so to me it's

more of a chore than recycling – recycling is quite low-level ... You can add that to your questions, would you consider it to be low-level, medium or high-level? [laughs] If I compare it with cleaning, which is not difficult but it's more time-consuming.

Poor follow-up – There are many problems with the extract below which yielded poor quality interview data. I started by asking a complex and double-barrelled opening question and then failed to follow up on the answer received. The exchange consists of one-line answers from Leon and too many questions from me (and I was following my interview guide too closely rather than listening to his answers). The continued use of the word 'OK' signals to Leon that his answers are sufficient, and it shuts down additional insights.

Katy: OK, let's move on to food preparation and we are quite interested in change over time, so we can start with your most recent meal, so it might be what you had last night, if you can tell me what it was you had and what was involved in preparing it?

Leon: I went to a pub and I had lasagne.

Katy: OK ... and how often would you go out to eat?

Leon: Probably twice a week, we usually cook at home about 4–5 times a week.

Katy: And what sort of meal would you be cooking if you were at home?

Leon: Depends what mood you're in really, curries, stir fries, roasts, doesn't really matter.

Katy: OK, can you tell me how you'd make a curry?

Leon: I'd use the paste, then I'd chop vegetables and fry them up, fry the meat then add it altogether and let it simmer away.

Katy: OK, and how long would that take you to do?

Leon: Probably an hour all in, to eat it too.

Katy: How do you share the cooking between yourself and your partner?

The power of silence

Silence is one of the most productive tools an interviewer has at their disposal. Often, nervous and novice interviewers rush to fill a silence with another question or comment. It is an easy mistake to make because in normal everyday conversation, we are used to filling silences and finishing off friends or colleagues' sentences. Resisting this temptation will give your participant space to continue to share their insights. A pause allows them an opportunity to gather their thoughts and a moment to think. Allowing silence within an interview serves as an effective probe, coupled with expectant body language from the interviewer such as nodding and making eye contact. This is a gentle way to signal to your participant that you want to hear more from them.

Silences that extend for too long, however, can be quite uncomfortable (see Activity 7.2). There is a delicate balance between a productive silence and an uncomfortable silence. Watching body language, such as your interviewee looking up as if to recall something, will help signal whether to allow the silence to continue. Katy will often count to five in her head and if nothing further has been offered by the interviewee, she will then move on with another question. When interviewing participants via online video-conferencing, be aware that silence can be caused by connection problems or by interruptions that are not obvious to the interviewer.

Do remember that sometimes what is *not* said can provide just as much information as what *is* said. Pay attention to silences or absences in your interviewees' accounts.

Activity 7.2

Experimenting with silence

The next time you have a conversation with a friend or colleague, play with the use of silence. Try holding a silence for a few seconds after they have finished talking and observe both your and their reactions to this. You will both probably feel quite uncomfortable with too much silence. You will observe how silence motivates people to fill it. Learn to be comfortable with some silence and experiment with different lengths of silence in the conversations you have over the coming weeks.

Active listening

Conducting an interview is an underestimated task, which goes beyond simply hearing what your participant says. Active listening is a real skill that requires intense concentration, not just on the words that are spoken but also their tone and implied meaning. It is equally important to pay attention to what is *not* said. Non-verbal clues such as body language can communicate a great deal. For instance, a woman Bethany interviewed about the ageing process said, 'I feel so frumpy' whilst pulling at her clothes, highlighting the discomfort she felt about the topic. Paying attention to body language is more challenging in an online interview because you will often only have access to your participant's head and shoulders. This makes it even more important for you to listen attentively to what is said and how it is said, as well as closely observe facial expressions. We discuss this in more detail in Chapter 8.

When actively listening, you should pay attention to the way people speak (the paralinguistic aspect of the interview) as this can offer important clues to an underlying meaning. For instance, intonation, pitch, anger, quietness and speed can all be important indicators of underlying meaning. Paying attention to adjectives (a word that describes a noun) and adverbs (a word that modifies a verb) can also be useful places to probe for further detail. For example, if someone said 'It was a wonderful holiday' or 'He shouted loudly', there is a clear emphasis in their speech. 'Wonderful' and 'loudly' are words which indicate that there might be more to the story than they could elaborate on. You might follow up with a further elaboration probe, such as 'You said it was a wonderful holiday; in what ways did you find it wonderful?' or 'You said he shouted loudly; could you tell me more about that?'.

You might also look out for clichés, such as 'Well, actions speak louder than words, don't they?' or 'My parents just don't understand me'. You could follow these with 'Could you elaborate more on that, please?' Finally, pay attention to words which are loaded. Some words are not just a word. When Bethany interviewed Shirley, she consistently repeated that she was 'reconciled' with her life, but the more she spoke, the less 'reconciled' Bethany thought Shirley truly was.

When listening within an interview, you are gathering communications on multiple levels and active listening takes a special kind of attentiveness. You are listening not only with your ears but also with your body, to your own reactions and responses, and even to your own thoughts as your interviewee speaks. You are paying attention internally as well as externally.

Activity 7.3

Practising active listening

There are several ways you can practise active listening and the sorts of skills needed to ask good follow-up questions before you conduct your interviews. Routinely reflecting on good and poor practice is the best way to make these skills more automatic:

1. Listen to a radio or television interview and as you do, make a note of the sorts of questions that the interviewer asks of the interviewee. What do you think of these questions? Would you have asked these questions if you were conducting a qualitative interview (note that journalistic interviewing is often more focused than research interviewing)? What other questions might have been asked that would have followed up on something the interviewee said? How do you feel about the topic under discussion, and is this influencing the sorts of follow-ups you want to ask?

(Continued)

2. Find a friend who is willing and prepare a short interview guide on a topic you know they will be interested to discuss (e.g. pets as part of the family, becoming a parent, how they practise their favourite hobby). Conduct the interview, listening very closely to what they say and paying attention to your own reactions. Listen carefully for phrases like 'You know what I mean' and be sure to probe fully. Notice how it feels to interview someone with whom you have a shared history – it may feel awkward to probe or you might feel at ease interviewing them. Reflect on this exercise and consult the good interviewing performance checklist to evaluate the quality of your interview (Box 7.4)

3. Visit the UK Data Service (https://ukdataservice.ac.uk) (or a similar online repository) and download an interview transcript. Go through the transcript carefully and look at the questions asked by the interviewer and the answers given by the interviewee. What do you think of their follow-up questions? Does the interviewer seem to adhere to key principles on the interviewing checklist (Box 7.4)? Can you find examples of things they did well and less well? Would you have asked the same follow-up questions? Prepare some alternative follow-up questions to the ones posed by the interviewer. You will notice that there are always lots of follow-ups that could have been asked but were not. This will partly be about the interest of the interviewer and their project, as well as missed opportunities to probe fully. It is often only once the transcript has been prepared that we can appreciate fully how much our participants have told us.

Box 7.4

Good interviewing performance checklist

- Take a few deep breaths and relax!
- Build rapport with your interviewee from the start of the interview
- Listen more than talk
- Probe fully
- Use silence
- Ask clear questions
- Allow participants to speak in their own words
- Don't interrupt your participant
- Be guided by the participant as to what they will talk about
- Keep track of what has been said and what has not yet been covered – this is not a normal conversation and you will be expected to steer it
- Don't move onto the next topic too quickly

- Don't assume you know what someone means by something
- Try not to comment with remarks like 'That's interesting' or 'How awful', as it can inhibit future responses
- Avoid too many extraneous remarks like 'OK', 'yes', 'right', 'hmm', etc. – they can be annoying for the participant and s/he might think that their answer is sufficient (see Katy's poor follow-up example in the Box 7.3 extract)
- Don't put words in the interviewees' mouth by finishing off their answer
- Refrain from summarising the interviewee's answer; the chances are it will be inaccurate or partial, or unhelpful – it is better to seek more depth (Yeo et al., 2014: 198)
- Avoid colluding with viewpoints which you strongly disagree with and instead maintain a neutral standpoint
- Watch for body language and tone of voice for cues of where to probe further
- Reflect honestly on what went well and less well after the interview, so you can improve next time.

Reflecting on the encounter

After you have conducted an interview, make an entry in your reflexive journal to capture your initial thoughts. This might include research-relevant notes about key points raised, your feelings about what was said, any areas you felt were not covered in the interview and how this information relates to your research question. It is helpful to include a basic summary of the content of the interview either in your journal or as a separate document. This summary will be helpful when you come to analyse your data and you can add more details to it once you have transcribed the interview.

It is also a good idea to reflect on the quality of your interviewing. Box 7.4 includes a list of key tips for conducting effective qualitative interviews. Assess your performance against these points. Box 7.5 includes several questions you can ask yourself about your interviewing style. You may find that you need to revisit these reflections once you have a transcribed version of your interview, as many of the small-scale interactions will not be easy to recollect. We would recommend going through the first few transcripts of your interviews closely to interrogate your interviewing style and learn from your good and bad practice. It is only by being honest with yourself about what has gone well and what has gone poorly that you will be able to improve.

Generally, you will know if an interview has gone well if you walk out feeling that your participant spoke for the majority of the time, you asked some good probes and you covered most of the themes in your guide. Interviewing can be an enjoyable experience for both the interviewer and the interviewee, but it can also raise difficult emotions for both parties. The next chapter focuses in on some of these more difficult emotional elements, as well as getting you to think about how your personal biography can affect how rapport is developed and about the way that interactions occur within this encounter.

Box 7.5

Questions to ask yourself about the quality of your interview

- What was your concentration and memory like during the interview? Were you really listening?
- How spontaneous, rich and detailed were the answers your interviewees gave?
- Were your questions brief compared to the length of their answers?
- Did you follow up on and clarify the points made by your interviewees?
- Did you use your guide flexibly?

Top tip summary

- A successful interview depends on the cultivation of key skills and qualities, such as curiosity, patience and empathy.
- You develop a good rapport with your participant by really listening to what they say and valuing their contribution to your project.
- Most interviews pass through five key stages and your role as an interviewer changes at each stage (see Table 7.1). In the early stages, put your participant at ease with low-stakes questions and take care to model the sorts of interaction you are hoping for in the rest of the interview. Questions that are key to your research question should come after these warm-up questions.
- Effectively managing the flow of an interview requires intense concentration and the practice of key interview skills, including using your interview guide flexibly, employing a range of different probing techniques and follow-up questions (see Table 7.2) and actively listening to your participant.
- Use the good interviewing checklist (Box 7.4) and key questions in Box 7.5 to judge the quality of each interview you conduct. It is only through practice and honest reflection on your performance that you will become an effective interviewer.

MANAGE THE ENCOUNTER

On completing this chapter, you should be able to:

- Reflect on how your personal biography can affect the data that is collected
- Assess how body language can affect your relationship with your participant
- Become attuned to the emotional dynamics in the research encounter.

In this chapter, you will learn how to reflect on your own interviewing practice and how your personal biography can affect the interview relationship. We consider the concept of impression management and that how we act in certain encounters can affect how people think about us – and in turn how this can affect the kind of data collected in an interview. We ask you to consider the different combinations of interviewers and interviewees and what difference they might make to the stories that are told.

By the end of this chapter, we hope you will have learnt how to tackle assumptions and reserve judgements that you might make about your participants. You will consider how body language can influence the relationship that is developed with your respondent, and how the partialness of body language (for instance, through telephone or online interviews) can create new challenges. This ability to reflect on your own positioning in the research encounter, and to also develop a sense of empathy by putting yourself in the position of your participant, will lead to more attuned interviewing skills. Accessing a person's story should be approached with care and sensitivity, and in this chapter we will emphasise the importance of trust and rapport for gathering rich data. This chapter will also look at how we interview on sensitive topics and how to manage those encounters.

Activity 8.1

Identity matters

Three researchers are conducting semi-structured interviews on the topic of the 'The Ageing Body':

- Researcher 1 is a 20-year-old heterosexual, White male from an affluent background interviewing a 60-year-old working-class woman
- Researcher 2 is a 58-year-old White female professor interviewing a 57-year-old Black woman who is educated to degree level
- Researcher 3 is a 42-year-old heterosexual female interviewing a 50-year-old gay man.

How do you think the biographies of the researchers and interviewees will affect the ways they relate to one another and the stories that are told?

Making a good impression

When we meet someone for the first time, they are likely to form an impression of our character. The interview encounter is no different. There will be visible characteristics such as our 'race' and ethnicity, our class, age, gender or visible disabilities which can affect how someone relates to us and we may find it hard to disguise or change these aspects of ourselves. Our choice of clothing, our accent or the formality of our vocabulary, or the openness of our body language and gestures, are all visible yet more subtle clues about our character. We may be able to adapt these to create a particular impression we want to give of ourselves. Then there are the invisible aspects of our background such as our qualifications, any hidden disabilities and our life experiences. These invisible aspects may be easier to conceal when trying to manage the impression we want to give of ourselves. However, they may still reveal themselves in unconscious ways when we meet with another person.

This first moment of meeting someone new is crucial and decisive. Willis and Todorov (2006) tested research subjects on their first impressions on a series of unfamiliar faces and the judgements that were made on that person's attractiveness, likeability, trustworthiness, competence and aggressiveness. They found that it took only 100 milliseconds for the subjects to make a judgement about the unfamiliar face that they were presented with.

When you first meet your interview participant, they will be forming an assessment of you which can shape the remainder of your interaction. Erving Goffman (1959: 1) wrote about *self-presentation* and *impression management* in his *dramaturgical theory*, first detailed in his book *The Presentation of Self in Everyday Life*. He argued that individuals are able to construct and manipulate their identity to create the desired impression in the presence of another person. He writes:

> When an individual enters the presence of others, they commonly seek to acquire information about him or to bring into play information about him already possessed ... Information about the individual helps to define the situation, enabling others to know in advance what he will expect of them and what they may expect of him. Informed in these ways, the others will know how best to act in order to call forth a desired response from him. (Goffman, 1959: 1)

How you present yourself to your interviewee therefore will make a significant impact on the way stories are told and interview data is created. Participants may be 'performing' an identity in order to elicit a desired response from you, such as sympathy; or in order to create a particular impression of themselves – for example, being 'fun', 'a victim' or 'a survivor'. These impressions will all shape the narrative in the interview.

Positionality

Positionality refers to how the researcher is positioned in relation to the social and political context of the study participants. It refers to dimensions such as our race, age, religion, culture, class, gender, political persuasion and sexual orientation. These dimensions affect our world view and how we construct our values, and this in turn influences how we conduct our research and the data that is produced. Our identity and that of our participant have the potential to impact the research process and the data collected. Bourke (2014: 1) writes: 'Identities come into play via our perceptions, not only of others, but of the ways in which we expect others will perceive us.'

Positionality affects all phases of the research process, from how we frame our original research question, to how we select participants, how we then relate to them in the interview process, and then how we write up and disseminate our findings. Rowe (2014: 628) writes:

> Not only do dimensions of culture, class, gender, age and political or social identity define the degree of commonality between researcher(s) and participants, but these dimensions extend into the values and world view that one brings to the research enterprise, thus influencing what is perceived and understood as knowledge.

If you have a lot in common with your participants, you might be considered an 'insider' and along with this, there might be common expectations and power equity. We tend to gravitate towards people who share similar views and it may feel more comfortable to interview people you are familiar with. But one of the difficulties with this is that you may become 'research-blind' to nuances in meaning. You may miss following up on points because they seem too obvious. Furthermore, your participants may omit things that they assume you already know or censor topics that they believe might damage the relationship between you. We spoke about this in Chapter 4 when we talked about the problems involved in interviewing friends.

Taking an 'outsider' role in research means that you do not share those dimensions with your research population, and therefore you are able to question and make sense of the taken-for-granted norms. But this is a more anxiety-provoking position to take and you need to build rapport with your participants in order for them to feel comfortable with you.

Moreover, because positionality is multidimensional you may identify with your participants on one level but not on another. For example, a White female researcher may be able to identify with her Black female participant from a *female perspective*, but not from a *Black female perspective*. An example of this is in Kimberley Huisman's (2008) research where she writes about her experience of conducting ethnographic research with Bosnian Muslim refugees, and although she was able to build friendships, develop rapport, and as a female, identify with the women she interviewed, she was also acutely aware of the differences in their cultures and world views.

Body language

When interviewing someone you should pay attention, not only to what they say, but also how it is said and the body language which accompanies it. Certain gestures can be used to encourage your participant to continue talking, such as leaning forward to express interest and attention, nodding, smiling and maintaining good eye contact. These show that you think what they say is valuable. Equally, body language techniques can be used to steer a rambling participant back on track, such as breaking eye contact, looking down or gently and respect-fully gaining their attention. Be mindful too that certain gestures can be loaded with suggestion – such as a nod or a shake of the head – and can lead to changes in how an interviewee responds. You should be mindful that certain body posi-tions can indicate defensiveness, such as crossed arms or a hand to your mouth, so you might need to be aware of how you are presenting yourself. Generally, in the course of an interview, you should try to match the interactional style of your participant.

Do note that gestures can be culturally relative so if interviewing across cultures, you may want to familiarise yourself with what is considered respectful for your participant and their community.

Case study 8.1

Body language as a source of data

Read through Bethany's field notes following an interview with a participant she called 'Bernice'. Take note of Bernice's body language and Bethany's emotional response to it.

Consider the dimensions of positionality between the interviewer and the inter-viewee. How do you think these factors affected the interview relationship?

Bethany: White British, cisgender female, aged 28. University PhD student and lecturer. Is a non-smoker and non-drinker. Has no children.

Bernice: White British female, aged 54. Achieved a degree as a mature student. Currently working in a therapeutic role. Has two children.

Bethany's field notes

I found Bernice quite intimidating and she appeared to want to take strict con-trol of the interview. She came across as a strong woman, with confidence, but which verged on arrogance. This was compounded by her body language, as she positioned a chair between us and sat with her legs pointing at me. During the interview, she drank gin and smoked, deliberately puffing her smoke in my direction. On the second visit, she sat down for dinner at the same time as I had been scheduled to arrive, eating without apology whilst I sat and waited. There was a sense of defiance there and I felt like she was communicating, 'Well, it is my house and I will smoke as much as I like, and I will eat and drink whenever I like'.

Just before the interview began, I wanted to write down some contact details that she insisted on giving me regarding another matter. Bernice snatched the pen

(Continued)

from me and insisted on writing things down for me – demonstrating her dominant behaviour and her attempt to gain control. She seemed used to being in control, later stating 'I've never really been very happy with authority'.

In the interview, Bernice seemed keen to impress me by introducing sociological and psychological theories that she had learnt in her own studies, in order to explain experiences from her life and how she felt about them, and she frequently framed her life story around a theoretical structure. She said, 'I ask questions like this at work'. This made me more nervous though because the more she said things like that, the more I felt she was monitoring my performance. As a result, my performance felt absolutely hopeless. I couldn't concentrate, empathise with her or feel anything but deep anxiety and impotence in her presence.

Dressing for an interview

Clothes can be important indicators about your character, and this can determine the degree of trust and rapport you build with your participants. There are certain clothes and accessories which might not be appropriate in an interview setting. For example, clothes that are overly revealing or flashy could be distracting or send inappropriate messages. Clothes which carry a political slogan might create tension. Clothes which are too formal, such as a suit, can create fear and suspicion amongst certain populations. You do not want to give the impression that you are from a completely different social reality. It is a good idea to match your clothing to what you anticipate your participants will be wearing, or to wear inconspicuous, low-key, neutral clothes which will blend into a group. You will also want to wear clothes which are comfortable to sit in for an extended period of time, and shoes that are comfortable to walk in if you have a long journey to the interview.

The partialness or absence of body language

In a post COVID-19 world, research interviews are increasingly likely to be conducted online via programmes such as Zoom, Google Hangouts, Facetime, Skype or Microsoft Teams. This approach to interviewing has its advantages in that it is more time-efficient and cheaper. However, telepresence is always partial and can have an impact on the interview relationship. Most notably, the absence of body language cues can change how we communicate with one another. We are likely to only see someone's face and shoulders, and sometimes only as a small image on a screen. This means that we are less likely to pick up on micro-cues in their body language.

Interviewing by phone also means a loss of body language to analyse and, as a result, it can feel quite difficult to build the same level of rapport with your participant. However, some interviewees may feel better able to open up in an online or telephone setting, because they are able to communicate from a place of relative anonymity, invisibility and security if they are in their own private space. This may particularly suit people who struggle to communicate co-presently, such as those who are shy or socially awkward.

Being reflexive

Depending on the aims of your interview, it can be really helpful to keep notes on your interviewees' body language, verbal and bodily expression, their use of the physical space, demeanour and presentation of self, and your own emotional responses to your participant. We recommend recording these immediately after each interview as it is easy to let your memories of the encounter slip. Bethany often makes audio recordings on her way home, of her impressions and feelings about each interview. We have stressed throughout this book the importance of keeping a reflexive journal. Frosh and Baraitser describe reflexivity as requiring the researcher to:

> keep an honest gaze on what s/he brings to the research process: how s/he sets it up, what is communicated to the subject, what differences of race, class, gender etc. might prevail and what impact they might have, and how her/his actions might influence the subject's own active meaning-making activities. (2008: 359)

As part of your reflexive practice, you might want to question 'why has this person said this?', 'why at this moment?' and, just as importantly, 'why did I respond in this way and how did it reflect in the interview?' (Roper, 2003: 27).

Interviewing on sensitive topics

Some topics are naturally more sensitive than others when it comes to interviewing. For instance, topics such as illness, bereavement, sexual behaviour, relationships or finances can all be difficult for your participant to talk about. Interviewing on sensitive topics can be a real challenge but also incredibly rewarding. Remember that if you have been thorough with your consent process and your interviewee is fully informed about the nature of your research, then there should be no real surprises for them with regards to what your topic is about. They will have agreed to take part, and if you ask the right questions, they will usually be ready to share their emotional experiences with you. You may find that many are willing to share more than you expect.

Managing emotions

Taking part in an interview, particularly on a sensitive topic, can be an emotional experience and it is not unusual for participants to react emotionally to some interview questions. Take a look through the scenarios in Table 8.1 and at how they might be managed.

Table 8.1 Managing emotional scenarios

Emotional scenario	Suggested strategies for managing it
Your interviewee starts to cry	Pause the interview for a moment and ask them if they would like you to turn off the recording. It might be that they would like to get a drink or a tissue and have a moment of time for composure before beginning again
	You should make ending an interview an available option to your participants – remember the ethical principle of *the right to withdraw*. You might like to ask whether the interviewee would like to reschedule the interview for another time or would like a follow-up phone call. It is also good practice to have some leaflets for professional support agencies in your bag, which you can offer to your participants if you feel their distress cannot be managed
An interviewee says something unexpectedly triggering for you, and you feel yourself becoming upset	It is important that you try your best to manage your emotions and focus on your interviewee's story. If your participant is already crying and you then cry a little with them, this is OK but try not to be the first one to cry as this could be disconcerting for your participant. Being able to contain and hold on to the emotional content of your participant's interview is a real skill. Following an upsetting interview, you might want to debrief with your supervisor about your experience but without breaking confidentialities. You should also reflect on the interview experience and consider why it was so upsetting, as this will give you a greater awareness not only of their story but also of the emotional baggage you are bringing to the interview
Your participant exclaims 'Ooh, this interview is just like free therapy!'	You should remember that you are not a counsellor and you should not pretend to be either. There are important differences between interviewing and therapy. The purpose of therapy is the facilitation of personality changes in a patient, but in a qualitative interview your aim is to obtain knowledge of the phenomenon under investigation, and any change in the interviewed subject is a side-effect (Kvale and Brinkman, 2009: 43)

Emotional scenario	Suggested strategies for managing it
An interviewee reveals a big secret to you and says, 'Oh, but I know you won't tell anyone'	As an interviewer, it can be tempting to search for sensational details and secrets in a story, however if material like this is revealed it is important to double-check your participant is still happy for it to be included in any analysis, even if they have already signed a consent form
	However, some secrets may take the form of information that reveals significant and immediate harm to another person. In that instance, you should speak to your participant about this and let them know you may need to involve an external agency, such as the police. However, this is a last resort and confidentiality should only ever be broken in very extreme and under specific circumstances
Your interviewee tells you a story that you can identify with and you want to share your story with them too	Oakley (1981) and later Hollway and Jefferson (2000, 2013) advocate for a more reciprocal exchange in the interview encounter, which builds rapport and creates intimacy. We too advocate sharing experiences in order to build rapport, but also caution against oversharing. We have found that oversharing can equally inhibit participants, making them feel embarrassed for sharing their story, or making them feel that their story is not being prioritised

The ethics of sensitive research

There are ethical questions which might be asked about this type of sensitive research. Should we do research which is potentially upsetting? Should we be provoking difficult feelings? Our response is that your participants have volunteered to take part and they have been fully informed as part of the consent process. Generally, they will know what to expect and they are usually prepared to speak about difficult experiences and feelings. In our experience, most participants find the session cathartic and they may not have had the opportunity to tell their story before. Bethany also found that conducting two interviews with each participant was a good strategy for managing deep emotions and distress, as she was able to revisit the participant a week later and discuss any concerns they had had following the previous interview. She would ask, 'How did you feel about that last interview?', 'How did you feel it went?' or 'Have you given any thought to what we talked about last time we met?'

Box 8.1

Vignette – Managing your emotions

You are interviewing a female survivor of childhood abuse. She recalls traumatic detail about her experience but does not cry. You begin to feel intense sadness and anger. Your interviewee is happy to continue talking about her experience, but you feel a bit overwhelmed and want to leave the interview.

(Continued)

What should you do? Choose THREE appropriate responses and if you are working as a group, discuss why the other responses might not be appropriate:

1. Cut the interview short. This is too much for you and you just want to go home
2. The participant starts to cry and then you cry a little too. You say, 'I know this is difficult and I can see this is upsetting for you. Thank you for sharing your story with me. Would you like to continue or take a little break while I make you a cup of tea?'
3. Listen to her talk but zone out. You don't want to feel those emotions so you look for any distractions you can in your immediate environment
4. Think hard about what you are feeling. You reflect on your feelings and realise that they give you an important clue as to how your participant feels about the situation
5. Listen to the interviewee talk, but when you get home you delete the interview because you cannot bear to transcribe it and listen to it again
6. Start crying before your research participant and excuse yourself to go to the bathroom. On your return, you ask the interviewee to move to a less sensitive topic
7. Listen without judgement. You recognise the intensity and significance of your emotional response, but you are able to remain calm and empathetic. You make the interviewee feel comfortable enough to continue with her story.

(*Suggested answers*: 2, 4, 7. It is important to remain emotionally (and physically) present and to provide containment for your participant's emotions; and you should reflect on your own emotional response.)

Box 8.2

Vignette – Keeping secrets

Bethany was interviewing 55-year-old Diane about her life story when she revealed a very deep, dark secret which not even her own daughters knew about. The only two people in the world who knew the secret were her and her husband. It would be potentially life-changing and shattering for her family if they were to find out. However, it fitted perfectly with Bethany's research.

After revealing the secret, Diane said, 'I am telling you this because I know you won't say anything'. Bethany had to gently remind her that she was conducting an interview, that Diane was being recorded and that she would be using her words as data for her research project. Diane waved off that information with her hand in a blasé gesture and wanted to carry on with the interview, revealing even more of the story.

Should Bethany:

a. Use this interview in its entirety with the secret included?
b. Use this interview with the secret omitted from the transcription, with a note that data had been removed for ethical reasons?
c. Not use the interview at all?

(*Answer*: Bethany chose route B as she deemed the secret too damaging to the family and although Diane had signed a consent form initially, it was unclear whether it gave Bethany explicit permission to mention this particular piece of information.)

Top tip summary

- Be aware of the visible and invisible factors which can affect the interview dynamics between you and your participant.
- Try to reflect on how your positionality can impact on the impression you give to your interviewee and the data that is subsequently collected.
- Try to notice the feelings that are aroused in you by an interviewee. How might these affect you and what might they tell you about the emotions of your respondent?

ADAPT YOUR STYLE (FOR OLDER PEOPLE, CHILDREN AND ELITES)

Learning objectives

On completing this chapter, you should be able to:

- Identify the key considerations when conducting qualitative research with particular groups of research participants – older people, children and elites
- Assess how power differentials within an interview can impact the research data collected
- Consider the use of physical space when interviewing older people in care homes or children in school
- Recognise the importance of gatekeepers in helping you to access at-risk populations
- Understand some of the strategies you can use to access hard-to-reach, elite populations.

There are particular groups of people who may require you to take extra care or employ special techniques in order to successfully and ethically interview them. This chapter will focus on the practical and ethical challenges of interviewing people in three distinct groups: older adults in residential care, children in schools, and elites in the workplace. We will demonstrate how you can adapt the interviewing styles you have already learnt to work with these populations. There will be practical tips on how to negotiate these more challenging research dynamics. We will provide case study examples drawn from our own research experiences of working with these particular groups.

Researching 'at risk' populations

There are a number of factors which can contribute to someone being considered vulnerable or 'at risk'. Vulnerability is a state of being in which the person is less able to protect themselves from harm, abuse and exploitation, which means that they are 'at risk'. The UK's Office of the Public Guardian safeguarding policy (section 5.2) has moved away from the term 'vulnerable' as it implies that some of the fault for the abuse could lie with the victim of abuse, and instead uses the term 'at risk' to refer to these populations (Office of the Public Guardian, 2017). Very broadly, people at risk can include (but are not limited to) those who are economically disadvantaged, living in poverty or who are homeless; people with disabilities, lack mental capacity or have an illness; victims of abuse; racial and ethnic minorities; those persecuted for their sexuality or gender; and finally, those who are considered vulnerable because of their age.

It is important to recognise that even if someone is considered 'at risk', it does not necessarily mean they are in any immediate danger or risk. It is important to balance out the duty to protect those at risk with their right to participate and have their voice heard in research. Being interviewed and participating in research can be empowering for some people, as they get to tell their side of a story which might get missed in official or more dominant forms of discourse. Researchers should not be unnecessarily protective and make assumptions about the ability of people to make rational decisions which are in their own best interests. As indicated in Chapter 5, respondents should have the option to refuse or withdraw participation in research, and if they feel fully informed about the research, they should have the right to participate, as long as there is no risk of harm to them.

Researching older adults living in residential care homes

Carrying out social research with older adults living in care homes requires the careful balance of protecting older people, whilst also making sure that the research is inclusive and hears the voices of an often-marginalised population. Assuming that a particular group of individuals, such as those living in care homes, are incapable of making the decision to participate in social research can deprive them of the right to have their opinions heard. Yet there still remains a balancing act of promoting the benefits of participation for older people, with the risks that might be involved.

By their very definition, care home residents will necessarily have some level of vulnerability. For older people in care, vulnerability may be a result of a mental or physical impairment, or arise from their social environment (in this case, the dependency that they have on the home and the staff within that home).

Gatekeepers

When you approach a research site, you will want to be inclusive and representative of the participants there, but how do you ensure that this is the case? Gatekeepers (discussed in Chapter 4) can help you identify who the various people are at the site and who it might be best to approach to be interviewed, but this may influence your sample selection. You should also be aware of coercive recruitment by gatekeepers. The ESRC ethical guidelines state that 'Research participants should take part voluntarily, free from any coercion or undue influence, and their rights, dignity and (when possible) autonomy should be respected and appropriately protected' (ESRC, 2015). This instructive also applies to when we want to interview 'at risk' groups who may have their participation mediated by a gatekeeper or other adult carer.

When researching in care homes, you must be mindful that some residents will not have the mental capacity to understand your research or to know what taking part will entail. Some residents may have the capacity but may be physically very unwell and taking part could be distressing. It is important to use a gatekeeper from the care home to help you to identify who would be the most appropriate people to approach. This could be a manager, a senior staff member or a relative.

Box 9.1

Stop & Reflect

Gatekeeper dilemmas

Question: What problem might you foresee happening if you ask a manager or staff member in a care home to select your participants for you?

Answer: The main problem you could encounter is *bias* and the *representativeness* of the residents in the home.

There may be bias in which care homes will allow you access in the first instance, but then once you have gained access to the care home research site, it is possible that the manager or staff member will suggest the most talkative of the residents in the home and also those who might give the most positive account of their life in that home.

Working within the Mental Capacity Act 2005

Although many of the older adults who live in residential care homes have the capacity to understand and contribute in an informed way to the research being carried out, others may be classed as more vulnerable and may be seen to lack the mental capacity to understand what is being asked of them. Defining the level of 'mental capacity' of an individual can be difficult, and indeed as a social researcher, you do not necessarily have the medical knowledge to make a judgement about the capacity of any particular resident to give consent. Furthermore, to *assume* a lack of capacity can be demeaning and unethical in its own right. Dobson (2008: 4) states: 'Researchers should assume that a participant or potential participant does have the capacity to decide whether to consent or not to their participation, unless there is evidence that questions the person's capacity to reach this decision'. In the UK, the Mental Capacity Act 2005[1] states that researchers should assume a person has the capacity to make a decision, unless there is proof that they do not have the capacity to make a specific decision, and that a potential participant must receive support to try to help them make their own decision. The potential participant has the right to disagree with the decisions that others (such as relatives or carers) might make (ESRC, 2015). It is important, therefore, to involve senior staff in care homes to help identify residents who will be best able to assist with the research. This, however, is less than ideal in terms of developing a diverse sample of residents. In Bethany's experience, care home managers, who have an interest in presenting an ideal image of their care home, may have a tendency to recommend the chattiest, liveliest, friendliest and most content residents, who will be able to give the most positive account of life in the establishment.

Another thing to consider is that mental functioning can be progressive or variable in older people living in care, particularly those with early signs of dementia. In other words, although you may begin an interview or series of research visits with an older person who is able to understand and contribute in a lucid way to start with, this state can change, particularly if a resident becomes unwell, tired or stressed in any way. As a researcher, it is important to be aware of changes in cognition, moment by moment. You should draw an interview to a close and inform a member of staff if you have concerns.

---

[1]The Mental Capacity Act 2005 is a piece of legislation which only applies to the UK, so if you are researching in another country you may like to look at what legislation applies to your work. However, the guiding principles of protecting vulnerable participants are likely to be comparable.

The Mental Capacity Act (UK) reiterates this protocol:

> During the course of conducting a project, researchers may become aware that participants who initially had given valid consent have lost that capability in later stages of the project. In order legally to conduct the research, the usual research process would need to be halted, the protocol revised, and ethical opinion re-sought before non-consenting participants could again participate (MCA, Section 34 (2)). (Dobson, 2008: 9)

In order for a resident to have the 'mental capacity' to consent, this means that a participant needs to understand that you are conducting a 'study' or piece of 'research' which will result in a 'report' or other 'research outputs' (book, website, presentation, article, etc.). They need to understand that they are being asked to 'talk about their experience or give their opinion', that they can say 'no' or 'stop at any time', and 'that this will not result in any detriment to them or the care that they receive'. It is important to phrase this information in an easy-to-understand yet informative manner, which is also non-patronising. Some residents may have previous experience of conducting research themselves in earlier years or may have taken part in other research projects, so may be very familiar with the research language, whereas others may not know key words such as 'research outputs' or 'informed consent' or 'withdrawal', so this will need explaining clearly and concisely.

Of course, research with individuals who do not have the mental capacity to give informed consent is possible but involves a more rigorous and external ethical process than can be offered at university level.

Box 9.2

Checklist – Consent to research under the Mental Capacity Act 2005

- Does the participant know that you are conducting a piece of research/doing a study/working on a project?
- Do they know what the project is about?
- Do they understand that you will use anything they say in research outputs – a report/a book/a university project/a presentation, or that what they say might be used by other researchers?
- Do they understand that you are asking them to give their opinion on something, or asking them to talk about their experience?
- Do they know they can say 'no' or 'stop' at any time and that this will not make any difference to the care they receive?
- Are they happy to take part and have they given you agreement (verbally or via a signed consent form)?
- Have they had a chance to ask you any questions?

Gaining informed consent from 'at risk' populations

As we saw in Chapter 5, informed consent to participate forms a crucial ethical principle. In interviews with 'at risk' groups, such as care home residents, and children in schools, you should make sure that any consent forms used with these groups are age-appropriate, simple and easy to understand, preferably with a series of boxes to be ticked, or, for children, with expression emojis (such as sad or happy) which can be circled.

If written consent is inappropriate or is hindering the relationship with the participant, then you can read out each section of the consent form and help them complete the form, whilst audio-recording the consent conversation. If a participant has a visual impairment, creating a consent form which is in a larger font or in braille might be appropriate.

Participants in 'at risk' groups may need additional time to process the details of the research project. It is good practice, particularly with these groups, to distribute an information sheet and perhaps even meet your participants informally at least a week in advance of an interview. The information sheet should be portable and timely. When you return for the second visit, you can double-check that they are still happy to participate now that they have had some time to read the information sheet and think about what participation might involve. When discussing the consent process, it is important to use accessible language.

Who should give consent?

Unless there are very exceptional circumstances, consent should be given by the research participant, wherever possible.

The term proxy consent refers to someone giving consent on someone else's behalf. Under the Mental Capacity Act 2005, proxy consent is not a lawful option under any circumstances. Adults who cannot make their own decisions for reasons of mental incapacity have to have a *best interests decision* reached for all decisions they themselves cannot make. In this case, you as the researcher would be required to seek advice from a consultee about what the participant's wishes might be, but they cannot legally offer consent (Health Research Authority, 2020b). Dobson (2008: 10) enforces this point: 'where adults lack the capacity to consent, the legal position in England and Wales is that no other person can be authorised to give proxy consent'. In everyday life, proxy consent happens, and you might hear the question 'does she take sugar in her tea?' being asked to a carer/relative without directly asking the question to the person in question. However, this is not an appropriate way to communicate, it is not technically lawful nor is it rights based, and it is certainly never appropriate in the research context.

As a researcher, you should be mindful of coercion and of participants being forced/or feeling obliged to take part in your research by another (usually a family member or an employer). We talk more about this in Chapter 4.

Physicality and the use of space in care home research

When interviewing older people in care homes, there may be physical barriers which affect how you conduct your research. First, these can relate to the physicality of the participant; you may find that some older people have visual, hearing or mobility impairments. You may find that you need to talk a little louder or to get physically close to someone's ear to be heard. This can create problems with maintaining confidentiality and privacy. For example, Bethany found that frequently saying 'Mmm' in response to a participant with hearing difficulties meant that he responded with 'what?' every time, which made the conversation very difficult. Similarly, those with visual impairments cannot always recognise an encouraging nod of the head or facial expressions which can build rapport. In this latter instance, it is more important to make encouraging noises such as 'Mmm hmm' or 'Yes', where appropriate, to indicate that you are paying attention.

Case study 9.1

Managing the physical space

92-year-old Mabel was rather hard of hearing and sat in her own chair in the communal lounge. She wanted to be interviewed there because that was 'her chair'. However, it became clear that having to speak very loudly to ask her questions, and with her responding in a loud voice, that her privacy was being compromised. Bethany suggested that they perhaps move to somewhere more private. Mabel agreed but insisted that the chair should come with her. However, the chair was an extremely heavy, electronic one with no wheels. Between two people moving the chair, and Mabel walking accompanied to the next room, it took them over half an hour to change locations!

If you are interviewing older people living in care then it is also important to be aware not only of mental changes, but also physical ones, and to report anything that you think is unusual. For instance, in one interview Bethany conducted, her participant began to complain of 'hot legs' that were 'burning', so Bethany checked that the participant was OK and wanted to continue, and then made sure that she reported this to the manager straight after the interview. Also watch for signs of tiredness, absence or irritability, which might indicate that you should gently draw the interview to a close.

Box 9.3

Stop & Reflect

Physical care and the care home interview

It is important not to make assumptions about someone's physical care or to intervene in any forms of treatment unless it is absolutely critical in that moment (in which case you should call for immediate help).

Multiple-choice question 1

When interviewing an older man in a care home, you notice bruising on his forehead and forearm. Do you:

a. Assume the bruising is a result of abusive practice and inform the Care Quality Commission immediately?
b. Keep an open mind and gently raise the concern with the care home manager after the interview, in a non-accusatory manner?
c. Assume that the person has had a fall and don't mention anything?

(*Answer*: B)

Multiple-choice question 2

An older female participant being interviewed in her private room in a care home, wants to do her diabetes check in your presence just before an interview starts. She tells you that her blood sugar levels are too high, but she wants to continue with the interview. Do you:

a. Offer to help her take a second test to double-check the results. How hard can it be to do a blood test?
b. Ignore the fact that her blood levels are high and simply carry on with the interview. You can't give her advice on diabetes.
c. Tell her that, with her permission, you will let the carer know that her levels are a little high, asking the carer to check in with her.

(*Answer*: C)

Box 9.4

Checklist – Advice for interviewing in care homes

- **Plan the order and phrasing of questions**: Think carefully about how you ask your questions. Keep the questions short and the phrasing simple. Ease into your interview by starting with a more informal discussion so that you build rapport with your participant. You might comment on the weather, or something interesting in the interview space, such as a photograph in a frame or art on the wall
- **Consider timings**: Consider the best time of the day to conduct an interview. You may want to consult with care staff over when busy periods are in the home, such as mealtimes, when visitors come in, or bedtimes. You will want to meet participants when they are at their most alert
- **Don't assume a participant's availability**: You might think that someone living in a care home is not busy and has ready availability, but their idea of being busy and your concept of busy might be very different. Some people living in care may prefer a very structured routine in their daily lives, and you will need to make sure you can fit around that. Always ask the participant when would suit them so that they can plan for your visit and perhaps put it in their calendar or diary
- **Organise the physical environment**: When interviewing in a care home, you will need to find a private space in which you will not be disturbed; this might be a bedroom or a private lounge space. Make sure that you inform a carer that you will be interviewing in that room. If a carer wishes to be present, you may want to ask them to wait outside of the room so that the participant's views can be heard without being biased by the presence of a carer
- **Monitor body language**: Look out for signs of fatigue, stress, confusion or illness. Pause the interview and perhaps arrange to return at another convenient time. When interviewing, make sure you maintain eye contact and have an open, relaxed body posture
- **Ask for help if needed**: If a participant asks for physical help, like transferring into bed from a chair, help with toileting or getting dressed, or if they ask for medical advice, then do not assist or advise them as you could end up accidentally injuring that person or misinforming them about a medical problem. Instead say, 'I will ask a staff member to come and help you with that'
- **Take precautions**: Be aware that interviewing in a private space can create risk for you as an interviewer. You are at increased risk of being falsely accused of inappropriate behaviour or physical risk if a participant's behaviour becomes unpredictable

(Continued)

- **Be careful with reimbursements**: You should give some thought as to how you will reimburse care home residents. Gifts of food such as chocolate could create a risk to those with certain medical conditions or allergies. Gift cards may be worthless if the participant is unable to go out to spend it. Money can also be problematic, causing tensions between residents, and it necessarily favours those who are well enough to participate, whilst disadvantaging those who cannot. Check with the home manager about what small gift might be appropriate for the individual resident
- **Limit the number of interviews**: Interviewing in a care home can be exhausting both for you and your participant. We would recommend a limit of three interviews a day. It can be particularly warm and cosy in participants' private rooms which may contribute to the fatigue
- **Consider the emotional impact on yourself**: In care homes, you may see, hear or even smell things that you do not experience in everyday life. This can be a shock sometimes. You may meet a resident who has serious or complex medical conditions, the sight of which can affect you emotionally. You need to be prepared for this, and remember to treat all participants with, what the renowned psychologist Carl Rogers (1959/1989) called, 'unconditional positive regard', which, within a counselling context, refers to accepting someone just as they are with no conditions attached.

Box 9.5

Guidance for communicating with people living with a disability

1. **Respect the person's autonomy**: Talk directly to the participant and not through a carer or relative.
2. **Mobility issues**: Do not assume that a person needs help; always ask if they require any assistance. Be mindful of a person's personal space and the space that they require to manoeuvre if they are using a mobility aid. Never reposition a person in a wheelchair without their explicit permission or request.
3. **Vision impairments**: Introduce yourself clearly if someone has vision loss. You may want to touch their arm to help them identify who is speaking. Let them know if you move around or leave the room. Never distract any accompanying service animal.
4. **Hearing impairments**: Speak with a normal tone of voice (avoid shouting). Minimise background noises where possible. If the person lip-reads then make sure you face the participant when talking to them, keep good eye contact and do not cover your mouth, if possible. If you need to wear a face mask, try to source one which has a clear cover over

the mouth, or wear a clear face shield instead. Make your questions short and simple. Consider writing the questions down, if this is appropriate. Be patient and be prepared to repeat questions. Be mindful of privacy if you have to speak louder.

5. **Speech difficulties**: Do not pretend to understand if you don't, instead ask the person to repeat what they have said. Consider using a communication board or talking mat, or asking them to write their answers down, if this is appropriate. Be patient, flexible and creative in the ways in which you communicate.

Sensory methods

Some older people with a degree of cognitive decline may find it hard to fully verbally express themselves in an interview. This is also true for individuals who might be discussing topics which are difficult and emotionally sensitive (as discussed in Chapter 8). There are interview techniques which you can use to enable that expression.

Buse and Twigg (2013, 2015) used a 'show and tell' method in their 'Dementia and Dress' project. This is a method that they called 'A wardrobe interview', which involved interviewing people with dementia alongside their wardrobes and using their clothing as a prompt for discussion. In these interviews, the researchers used objects to help reveal the life story of their participants. They showed how objects, in this instance clothes, can conceal or reveal our identity. They recognised that there is often a story behind an item of clothing. For example, someone might say, 'this was the jacket I was wearing when X happened'. The touching of the fabric is sensory and tactile, and through this sensory elicitation (Pink, 2009) the participant is able to capture a richness of memories which might have been missed through simply talking to that person.

Another technique that you could use is object elicitation, whereby you invite participants to bring an object to the interview which means something to them and then reflect on that object during the interview. Photo elicitation can be used in the same way, with photos brought in by the participant or introduced by the interviewer.

Researching children in school

It is only in relatively recent years that research has included children as active participants in the research process. Darbyshire (2000) argues that research has been predominantly conducted *on* children rather than *with* and *for* children, and that research has tended not to view the child as an active agent. Alderson (2019: 58) writes: 'If researchers are to understand and support the children's best interests, they have to re-theorise childhood, to take children's own views seriously and respect even young children as competent research participants'. However, changes in the safeguarding policy frameworks for children, such as the United Nations Convention on the Rights of the Child 1989 and the Children's Act 2004, have resulted in changes in how we view children. In research now, children should be viewed as having their own agency, have a say in their participation and have the ability to own the expertise of their experience (Fargas Malet et al., 2010). You might want to involve children in many of the stages of the research process, from the planning and formulation of research questions, to how the data is collected and disseminated.

Gatekeepers in school

Adult gatekeepers, such as teachers, group leaders, parents, social workers or guardians, will usually mediate access to children for research. It is important that any mediating adult introduces the child to the research, rather than volunteering the child's cooperation without any real explanation being given to the child. When researching in school, gatekeeping might take place at a number of levels, such as gaining access from the headteacher, teacher, parent and child. This can be a time-consuming and sometimes complex process.

You also need to be mindful of coercion when working with at-risk groups such as children. Coercion is a pressure to participate and can be intentional or unintentional. For example, a child being interviewed at school might feel coerced to participate in the research as a result of peer pressure, parental pressure, pressure from the teacher, or from you as the researcher. This could be intentional – the teacher or parent might say, 'Oh, come on, it will be fun, all your friends are taking part', or it could be unintentional, with the child wondering whether their grades will suffer if they decline. Due to the differential power relations between an adult and a child, once a mediating adult has given consent for the child's participation, the child might find it difficult to withdraw from the research. It is therefore important to ask for the child's assent to participate in addition to acquiring the consent of the adult.

Box 9.6

Stop & Reflect

Over-researching 'at risk' populations

As a researcher, you should be mindful that some at-risk groups can be over-researched because they are easy to define and convenient for access. Read the following vignette and answer the questions that follow.

Vignette

Goldhayes Primary School is located next door to a university. Every year, the headteacher is approached by university students on a Sociology of Education module, who want to conduct research with the teachers and pupils at the school. The first time the school was asked, the headteacher granted access to three students who planned to interview teachers and observe the class. However, one of the students was unreliable and didn't turn up when expected, keeping a teacher and class waiting.

Discussion questions

1. How might the headteacher feel about being approached every year by a new group of students wanting to conduct research in her school?
2. How might the unreliable student have spoilt the field (of the school) for future students?
3. How might the teachers feel about having their classes observed, and being interviewed by university students?

Multiple-choice question

What could be done to stop the school becoming over-researched? (Select TWO correct answers.)

1. The university course director could come to an agreement with the headteacher about the number of students who can approach the school each year
2. The raw data collected by students in previous years could be made available to future students (with the correct re-use permissions on the consent form)
3. Students could only speak to teachers when they have left the school after work.

(*Answers*: 1 and 2)

Consent and assent with children and adolescents

Children are generally considered an 'at risk' population who are unable to give fully informed consent. Usually, parental consent is required for children to take part in research, but you should also seek the child's 'assent'. Assent is agreement from someone who is not able to give legal consent to participate in the research.

At the age of 16, a child can consent to medical treatments without parental knowledge or agreement. The Gillick principle, or Gillick competency, as it is sometimes known, is sometimes used to assess whether a child is mature enough to make their own decisions and understand the implications of their decisions. Under the Gillick principle, if a child understands what is involved in the medical procedure (or more widely, what is involved in the research) and is willing to take part, then parental consent would not be necessary. However, it would be a rare exception to proceed without parental or a legal guardian's approval.

When gaining assent from children, the research must be explained in clear and simple terms. Let them know what will happen. Let them know that they can withdraw without getting into trouble. Ask them if they want to continue. If they do not want to participate then do not include them, even if you have parental consent. You might consider providing children with verbal and non-verbal ways of confirming their assent, such as showing them pictures which represent a happy and a sad face to show them their options.

Voice and autonomy

When working with populations who are vulnerable or at risk, it is particularly important that you respect and protect their autonomy and help make their voices heard. You should practise empowering research, and your research should add value to the lives of your participants.

When working with children in school, they may view the interview as schoolwork and view the interviewer as a teacher. As a result, the child may feel they have to give correct answers to your questions. You can minimise this by reassuring the child that there are no right or wrong answers to the interview questions. Often, a responsible adult is nearby during an interview, but you should try to keep the interview confidential and not allow the adult to influence, bias or inhibit the discussion.

Once in an interview, a child may refuse to take part or to talk, or may even become upset. You can use this as a signal of withdrawal from the interview. The child should not feel pressured to continue. You should try to end the interview on a positive note, and do not make the child feel bad for wanting to leave the interview.

Physicality and the use of space in school

When researching with children in school, you may also get similar requests to be involved in physical care, such as toileting or help with dressing, or even have a child ask for a cuddle. In all of these instances, you should seek the support of one of the teachers and not take it upon yourself to be involved in any activities which involve the personal care of the child.

In terms of organising the physical environment in school, there may be limitations in terms of timetabling and finding space in a room to conduct your research in (Kellett and Ding, 2004). Bear in mind that some spaces may have negative connotations for the child, such as 'the headteacher's office', where they may have been sent when misbehaving. Instead, there may be spaces in the school which 'represent an in-between of the formal and informal worlds of the school' (Fargas Malet et al., 2010: 178) such as activity or art rooms, or resource rooms, which can make for suitable interviewing spaces.

Child protection

In the unlikely event that a child discloses information that raises concern about their welfare or about immediate significant harm to another, you should try to persuade the child to talk to those involved, but, if this is not possible, then you may have to break confidentiality. You may need to have up-to-date Disclosure and Barring Service (DBS) clearance, if you are researching for a prolonged period of time with children. A DBS check looks at your background to ensure that you do not have a criminal record and that you do not pose a risk to children. If any other safeguarding disclosures arise in an interview, it is important to raise these with the gatekeeping, mediating adult (i.e. the headteacher in the context of a school, or the safeguarding lead), who will be able to refer to the appropriate safeguarding procedures, which include (but are not limited to): The Children and Families Act 2014, The Children Act 2004, The Safeguarding Vulnerable Groups Act 2006, as well as local authority safeguarding frameworks and the school's own policies.

Interviewing through art and play

Creative techniques such as drawing, painting or modelling can be used alongside interviews to elicit discussions, particularly when interviewing children. Children often talk more freely when engaged in activities such as art or play, as it opens up a new space free from the constraints of existing norms and expectations (Brown and Leigh, 2019). Art can be a fun activity for children and can open a space for them to express their views or tell their story whilst engaging with the task. Sometimes what the child says whilst drawing can be as revealing as what they actually create (Kegerreis, 2009).

Creating art together can also be used as an ice-breaker activity, helping to establish rapport with the child. Guided drawing, such as 'can you draw your house for me?', can create a trigger and help the child organise their thoughts over a particular narrative for the interview. Similarly, play with creative toys, such as threading beads or playing with a dolls' house, can help a child create a narrative for their interview.

Dolls' house play can help the child re-enact the experience they want to tell you about. Talking with a child whilst they play can feel less threatening and direct than sitting face to face for an interview. Through play and art, the child is given more control over the interview and the space in which they are being interviewed.

Whilst the child is talking, it is important for the researcher to continue to give verbal prompts such as 'can you tell me more about that?' and non-verbal cues that they are listening such as nodding the head, smiling or maintaining eye contact. Cameron (2005) warns against using exclamations such as 'Great!', 'Terrific!' or 'Cool!' as they 'may discourage the child from telling the whole story which includes the "non-cool" parts!' (Cameron, 2005: 603; Fargas Malet et al., 2010).

Creative techniques do not just have to be used with children; for instance, Brown and Leigh (2019) used these techniques in interviews with adults on the topic of higher education research. Leigh writes evocatively about the experience:

> When my first participant arrived and saw the studio space; which was bright, with windows looking out onto green lawns, blue skies, a clean wooden floor and with a scattering of cushions, three different colours of A3 size paper, oil pastels, graffiti double-brush pens, charcoal and pencils, she said that it felt more like a playdate than an interview. In a sense she was exactly right, and the phrase 'playdate' seemed evocative of the essence of joy, creativity and play that I wanted the participants to engage in with me as they explored whether and how their embodied practice shaped their identity and academic work. (Brown and Leigh, 2019: 7–8)

Brown and Leigh's (2019) research resulted in multimodal data which included interview transcripts, drawings, video footage and a reflective journal. The authors found that this resulted in rich, varied data and an enjoyable, honest research experience (2019: 7–8). They argue that focusing purely on textual data created through interviews can be restraining and restrictive, allowing us to only see 'one idea of the world, the one in which words are the most valued way of communication' (2019: 64). By acknowledging multi-modal forms of collecting data such as through art, music, drama, and so on, as researchers we can become more open to new forms of communication which are often beyond words.

Researching those in positions of power (elite groups)

The elite or expert interview represents a particular set of challenges. Students can be apprehensive about researching those in positions of power, but it is worth remembering that power imbalances are common across all types of interview. Think, for example, of Bethany's encounter with Bernice, described in Chapter 8 (Case study 8.1). The research process does not represent an equal encounter, regardless of whether the interviewee is characterised as an elite. The interviewer has the authority to select and reject data though different stages of the research process, such as designing interview questions, selecting participants and writing up findings (Letherby, 2003). However, interviewees are not powerless because they can deny or allow you access, they can refuse to answer questions, or they can only tell you part of the story or not tell the truth (Sharff, 2010).

In textbooks on interviewing, the elite or expert interviewee is usually described as being more powerful than the researcher because of their position in society and/ or the knowledge that they hold. For example:

> Elites are those at the top of the social, political or economic hierarchy. They are the CEOs of companies, the very famous, the very wealthy, people of great prestige and/or accomplishment. Some have climbed the ladder of success themselves; others were born into wealth and social position. They are used to being in control. [...] Technical experts are those who have access to specialised knowledge, such as management skills, computer expertise, or esoteric scientific information. Like elites, they want to focus an interview on subjects they know best. (Rubin and Rubin, 2012: 175–6)

Whilst we agree with Rubin and Rubin's definition of the characteristics of elites or experts, we are more cautious in assuming that they are always more powerful than the researcher. Like Smith (2006), we think of power in the interview as being more mobile and diffuse. Just because someone holds power outside of the interview, it does not mean this will automatically translate to the interview encounter. Indeed, both of us have been interviewed as experts and can attest that we did not feel powerful in these encounters – rather, we were apprehensive and worried about whether we were giving the interviewee the information they needed!

Having said this, our experiences of interviewing experts and elites point to some commonalities when it comes to gaining access, negotiating consent and attribution, and managing the interview encounter, that we think will be helpful to you.

How to access elite/expert interviewees

Most of the techniques described in Chapter 4 about recruiting participants apply to elite/expert interviewees. The main difference with this population is that you are likely to both make more extensive use of gatekeepers (by using existing networks and name dropping, for instance) and be managed by various gatekeepers (such as secretaries and agents) when trying to access and convince elites/experts to participate. Just as with the other two populations described in this chapter, it is important to reflect carefully on the influence gatekeepers have on the data you can collect.

There is no magic formula for accessing elites or experts, but persistence and luck are likely to be key factors in your success. One thing that can be said about this group is that they will often have public profiles and will therefore be easily searchable through online networks like LinkedIn or organisational websites. If you use LinkedIn, you should spend some time on your own profile so that potential interviewees can check you are who you say you are. Katy has had some success in securing interviewees by using LinkedIn direct messaging, which can be accessed by upgrading to a paid membership.

Another way to find potential expert or elite participants is to be on the lookout for conferences and conventions where you know that policy makers, experts or government officials are likely to visit. This might be a cost-effective way of accessing many interviewees at once if you can attend and find time to talk to people between seminar sessions (though do be aware that time may be limited as interviewees will need to be at particular events during a conference).

It is especially important to get right your initial contact letter or email to an elite/expert interviewee, so be sure to look at our advice on writing one of these in Chapter 4 (Box 4.5). The introductory letter should demonstrate your credibility as a researcher and allay any doubts or fears about your intentions. When you are trying to negotiate access and in early discussions, you should be clear that you are not a reporter or interested in exposing a scandal, for instance. Your academic interest or credentials might be demonstrated by sending them examples of your existing research or signposting them to a supervisor or project website so they can check you out.

Snowball sampling is common in elite and expert interviews and it can be a good idea to use existing secured interview contacts to identify potential future participants. If you name one of your interviewees to secure another interview, you should be sure that you have their permission to do this and that this interviewee is aware that this will compromise their anonymity in your study.

Another point to bear in mind when arranging interviews with elites, is that interviews can be moved without much prior notice. Katy once arrived at a scheduled interview in Brussels only to be told that her interviewee had a pressing appointment that meant her interview had to be postponed. Fortunately, she was staying in Brussels for a week, so it was possible to reschedule for later that week.

Table 9.1 Do's and don'ts when trying to access elites and experts

Do	Don't (or try not to)
• Spend time researching the names of people you want to interview	• Address emails/letters with 'Dear Sir/ Madam'
• Try to directly contact your potential interviewee by guessing their email address (do a Google search to see if you can find the format the organisation uses) or messaging them via LinkedIn	• Use a generic contact email (though sometimes there really is no choice)
• Use institutional email addresses or headed paper to demonstrate your academic credentials in your introductory email/ letter. This might also mean including your supervisor's name (or your own if you have already published in this field) so that potential interviewees can check out your or your supervisor's profile online	• Be un-searchable online or have a poorly populated profile on LinkedIn
• Follow up your initial contact with another email or phone call after a week, and be systematically persistent (see Case study 4.1 in Chapter 4)	• Assume that because you haven't received a reply after your first or second attempt, this person does not want to be interviewed
• Make use of established contacts and existing networks to assure your interviewee that you are legitimate and can be trusted, e.g. 'name-drop' where appropriate	• Make promises of anonymity to existing participants to secure another interviewee
• Know when to give up and move on to another potential participant	• Persist in contacting someone who has consistently ignored your emails or refused to talk to you on the phone. Remember that everyone has the right to refuse to participate

Issues of consent, anonymity and attribution

Elites and experts are often being interviewed on behalf of an organisation they represent rather than as an individual. This can make them wary about how their words might be publicly represented, especially if they have had a bad experience with a journalist previously. They may be concerned that their words will be used to damage the reputation of their company/organisation/brand, so you must carefully negotiate issues of consent, anonymity and attribution with them before and after you have conducted the interview.

Once you have secured access, it is a good idea to send the consent form and information sheet in advance so that your participant can check through these. At the start of the interview, you should expect to go through these forms, but Katy often finds that elites do not wish to sign the form before they know what they have said. She now anticipates this and includes a disclaimer that they do not have to sign the form until the end. She also reassures them that anything they do say in the interview can be removed from the transcript if they are unhappy with it. This usually works to allay any fears that their words might be used against them.

Katy tends to offer elites the opportunity to see their interview transcript as standard, and it will sometimes happen that interviewees come back to her to ask her to change or omit something. It is a good idea to ask them why they want to make the changes, and to keep old and new data to see what changes there are. Obviously, you would not be allowed to use any data they have withdrawn but it might inform your understanding of your research area if you find that certain topics are consistently missing from people's accounts, or to learn where there are sensitivities.

Box 9.7

Reasons why someone might want to change their transcript

- They may be embarrassed about what they said
- The event/situation has changed since
- They may have had a genuine change in opinion
- There may be pressure from an authority figure.

Offering to share the data you have collected about someone is both a courtesy and their right, but this becomes more important with elite or expert interviews because of the issues of anonymity and attribution. Often, it is difficult to anonymise the contribution of elites or experts because there are so few people who hold these positions (for example, if you are speaking with a representative from a specific organisation or government department), or your interviewee is one of a very small pool of people who has specialist knowledge. This means that you must carefully negotiate the terms on which you can use the data collected.

Katy asks her interviewees both whether they wish to remain anonymous and want their organisation to remain anonymous. Sometimes, participants ask for anonymity on both counts, but more often they want their organisation and name represented. She will also ask her participants whether she needs additional consent to attribute any quotations from the interview or if they give her free rein to quote anything they have said in the interview. Participants have occasionally said that she cannot attribute any quotation without their prior agreement but, more often than not, participants have been happy for her to attribute everything after having seen their transcripts.

For particularly sensitive topics or where participants have asked for anonymity, you will need to think carefully about how you will present your data. If you think complete anonymity is not possible, you should include this in the consent forms and information sheets. A possible way of anonymising contributions where there is a limited pool of people, is to create composite narratives. For example, when Willis (2018) was interviewing MPs about climate change, she developed typologies of typical responses to create four fictional participants that amalgamated the data from several participants. This protected the identities of the limited pool of MPs she spoke with, whilst also staying true to the data collected.

Another thing that could happen is that there may be observers in the room with you when you conduct the interview, especially if there are concerns about how the data might be publicly represented, or fear of damage to a brand. When interviewing a CEO of a company in China for a documentary she was making for the Open University, Katy was surprised when three other people sat in on the interview and were making comments about the answers given (which Katy could not follow as the interpreter only relayed some of the information).

You may think that because you are interviewing powerful people, you do not have to worry so much about ethics. The consent procedures are often more of a process of negotiation when you are interviewing this group because the data collected tends to be from individuals and organisations who are in the public eye. Although in our experience it can take a little longer to deal with these issues, we maintain that it is important to treat all participants in research with respect, regardless of the power they possess outside of the research encounter.

Key things to consider when interviewing experts or elites

Activity 9.1

Interviewing experts or elites

Imagine that you have secured an interview with the government minister for the Department of Education to discuss a recent change in educational policy. It was made clear to you at the time of organising the interview that there is a limited window for the interview between two other appointments. Either on your own or in groups, list the things you should do to prepare for this interview. How might you be able to quickly establish rapport and ensure that you get the minister speaking candidly about the topic in the time you have?

Elites and experts tend to be quite used to being interviewed and giving their opinions on topics. This can mean that they try to steer the interview in the direction they want and avoid answering questions they do not wish to. This type of participant tends to be busy, so there is almost always a limited time for the conversation, and you will likely only see them once (though you may be able to follow up by email). With these factors in mind, Box 9.8 summarises some of the ways you can prepare for an interview with an elite/expert to get the most out of the encounter.

Box 9.8

Checklist – How to prepare for a time-limited interview with an elite/expert

- Send the participant information sheet and consent form in advance of the interview to hopefully save some time at the start of the interview
- Send interview questions, if requested (we recommend sending key themes rather than fully worded questions)
- Do your homework and do not waste their time with questions that you can find answers to online or in other relevant documents
- If you are interviewing on a specialist topic, be sure you are familiar with key terms and jargon – this will show your participant that you are serious about the topic and their time
- Only ask a limited number of key questions
- Prepare your questions to get around rehearsed answers.

Every year, we run a summer school at the University of Essex and every year our students ask us how to get elites to truthfully answer their questions and move beyond rehearsed answers. There are a number of techniques you can try but it is worth being aware that getting some groups of people to talk candidly to a researcher is very challenging. The most important thing we think you can do is to spend a lot of time researching your participant before the interview so you are well aware of how they have responded publicly to the issue you will be interviewing them on (or, if they have never spoken on this topic, you can get an idea of the sorts of things this person is well known for). Then you can use this information to help you to create a list of questions that is tailored to this participant. Try not to phrase questions in a way that will encourage a rehearsed or institutionalised response – for example, if you know that a government department consistently represents an issue in a particular way, do not phrase your question to get that pro-forma answer. Instead, you could indicate that you are aware of the existing position and rather ask about the story of how they arrived at that position or way of working.

Another way to avoid rehearsed answers is not to send fully worded questions in advance of the interview. Katy is often asked for a list of interview questions when she arranges interviews with organisational representatives, but she tends to send a list of key topics the interview will cover rather than the questions. Bethany once sent the questions in advance to a participant, and on arriving at the interview was given a piece of paper with typed answers, which she quickly had to read and then encourage her respondent to elaborate around.

Other tools at your disposal are the techniques we have already outlined in Chapters 7 and 8 – making good use of elaboration probes, looking for body language and paying attention to places where people might be defensive in what they say. Also, make a note of what is not said in the interview if a particular topic is consistently absent or participants find it difficult to talk about something, because this could be important once you have collected all your interview data.

Top tip summary

- When researching at-risk groups, ensure you create a balance between promoting the benefits of participation and empowerment versus the risks involved.
- Be aware of coercive recruitment techniques when working with at-risk groups.
- Be alert to cognitive and behavioural changes in your participant when working with older people or those living with a disability.
- Consider using creative interview techniques such as art and play to communicate with groups such as children, who may find it harder than adults to express themselves in a verbal way.
- For all the interview types discussed in this chapter, it is important to carefully reflect on the impact that gatekeepers might have on shaping the access you have to potential participants.
- Spend time crafting your introductory email/letter and update your public online profile when you are trying to gain access to elites/experts. It is important to demonstrate your credentials as a genuine academic researcher.
- Be prepared to negotiate the terms on which you can use or attribute data collected in an elite/expert interview.
- Do your homework when preparing interview questions for elites/experts, so that you can make best use of the time you have with them.

10

TRANSCRIBE YOUR DATA

Learning objectives

On completing this chapter, you should be able to:

- Identify different ways data can be transcribed
- Decide on an appropriate style of transcription for your project
- Create high-quality transcripts
- Evaluate who should do the transcription.

Transcription is the process of turning your audio or video recordings into a textual form. It is a key stage of the research process as it provides a transparent, contextual and documented record of your research. It is a key stage in the analytical process, allowing for a systematic review of the content; you should be able to search your transcripts and easily retrieve information from them. High-quality transcripts help you to adhere to ethical protocols as you should have a consistent approach to anonymisation which accompanies or follows the transcription process. Finally, if you want to share your data beyond the original research project, then it should be presentable and independently understandable by a third party. In this chapter, you will learn how to transform your audio-recorded interview data into high-quality written transcripts. We consider different transcription styles and how to match the style to your theoretical approach. We evaluate the options on who should do the transcription – do it yourself, pay a professional transcription service, or use an automated software program. Finally, we show the importance of clear file naming and keeping your transcripts safe.

Transcription styles

When transcribing your data, you may be surprised to discover how messy our speech is. In everyday conversation, we tend to speak in broken sentences and repeat ourselves. We pause, we demonstrate emotion and we might use slang, swear words or colloquial terminology. You must make decisions therefore about how much of this to capture when typing up an audio recording. How 'clean' do you want your data to read? And how much of the authenticity is lost when you clean it? Transcription styles can range from a full verbatim transcription which is most like natural speech to intelligent verbatim which is the most like written language.

You will soon discover in the process of transcribing your own data that it is not as straightforward as it first seems. You need to think about what aspects of the recording you want to keep and which to omit. Do you really want every single 'Mmm' in your transcript? Perhaps that little agreement signal 'Mmm' is really important in the context of your particular research or that specific interaction. However, in other projects that 'Mmm' holds little significance. Kvale (1996: 165) likens this process about deciding what needs to be kept or omitted in a transcript to the creation of a map. He writes:

> Transcribing involves translating from an oral language, with its own set of rules, to a written language with another set of rules. Transcriptions are not copies or representations of some original reality, they are interpretive constructions that are useful tools for given purposes. Transcripts are decontextualized conversations, they are abstractions, as topographical maps are abstractions from the original landscape from which they are derived. Maps emphasize some aspects of the countryside and omit others, the selection of features depending on intended use.

On some maps, it will be important to the creator to include every landmark in the area, and on other maps the focus might be on where rivers and lakes are situated. It will depend what you want to use that map for. In the same way, you need to make a decision about the focus of your transcription. What will you include? What will you want to do with that transcript? And how will you want to analyse it?

Box 10.1

Stop & Reflect

Full verbatim versus intelligent verbatim

Compare these two examples of transcription.

Question   Which style of transcription would be most suited to your research purposes? Why?

Full verbatim example

Petra: So ... um, [sighs] we are a single parent family, you know, and Eddie is almost fourteen years old and I- I'm, like, nearly 51 and we've lived here for ... lemmie see ... almost fourteen years, we moved in just before Eddie was born and we've always been interested in recycling really. [Pause] Um, my mum was—she's passed away now, like, but um, sh- she was re- recycling when it was considered a bit wacky and hippyish, you know?

Note: As you can see, all the filler words like 'um' and sounds like thought pauses, for instance 'lemmie see', slang words such as 'hippyish', repetitions and all other expressions, have been transcribed exactly as they have been heard.

Intelligent verbatim example

Petra: We are a single parent family and Eddie is almost 14 years old and I am nearly 51 and we've lived here for almost 14 years, we moved in just before Eddie was born and we've always been interested in recycling really. My mum's passed away now but she was recycling when it was considered a bit wacky and hippyish.

Note: As you can see here, all fillers, thought pauses, repetitions and all other expressions have been omitted. The text is much neater and more like written text. It is easier to read but it loses some of the sense of authenticity and character of full verbatim transcription.

(Credit to wordbee.co.uk who transcribed this part of Katy's data and provided the descriptors.)

It is possible to transcribe somewhere between full verbatim and intelligent verbatim, perhaps just capturing certain features and not others (just like the map creation). But the key message here is that you need to be consistent across your data set and have a clear justification for why you have transcribed in this way.

The other thing to consider when transcribing is whether you need to capture any additional descriptions or emotional responses. Do you want to capture your participant crying, laughing or even sneezing? Do you want to record interruptions or the fact that a dog barked in the background? How important are these descriptions to your analysis? Do you want to write how you feel emotionally at a particular moment in the interview, in response to something your participant has said? As a psychosocial researcher, Bethany makes a note of as many descriptors as she can, particularly emotional responses. It is important for her analysis that she can recognise her participant's emotional reactions to certain topics. Take a look at Box 10.2 (Mary's interview) and note how Bethany has included the participant's emotional responses in the square brackets. Bethany always uses [square brackets] to contain these extra emotional responses and she reserves {curly brackets} for any anonymisation.

Box 10.2

Capturing emotional content in transcription

Mary: Um, this is the sticky bit. This is the bit I was hoping you were going to forget about. Until recently I have always thought I was fine. I will probably get all emotional, I thought I was fine, but I don't know what has happened just [emotional tone and about to cry] recently but I feel that I am not going to age as gracefully [laughing] as I thought I might. Not that I have any objections to ageing disgracefully, actually I quite fancy doing that [laughing].

How you transcribe is dependent on the methodological approach you are taking in your research. A psychosocial approach will most likely use an intelligent verbatim style as it captures emotional content such as authenticity of voice and micro-indicators of where unconscious defences might be revealed. However, this layer of detail may not be so important for a social policy focused interview with a representative from a professional organisation. When transcribing 'elite' interviews, there may be an expectation that you 'tidy up' the spoken language into a full verbatim style to present a more professional image of the organisation and its representatives.

The way people interact through speech can also be revealing of social behaviours, and forms the theoretical and methodological basis of an approach called conversation analysis. Conversation analysis (CA), developed by Harvey Sacks, Emanuel Schegloff and Gail Jefferson in the late 1960s and early 1970s, examined social interaction through turn-taking speech (Sacks et al., 1974). CA requires a very specific form of data analysis which requires a very precise transcription process, which aims to capture the speech almost exactly as it was said. Transcription in CA captures the minute level of detail in speech, including things like intonation, speed, pauses and overlapping speech between two or more people. Activity 10.1 provides an example from a police caution interview, taken from Elisabeth Carter (2013: 81).

Activity 10.1

Conversation analysis transcription key

The following key and transcript have been taken from Carter, E. (2013) *Analysing Police Interviews* (Bloomsbury), showing data transcribed using CA.

Using the key below, try and read this transcript out loud exactly as it was said in real life. Notice how it sounds more like real-life speech.

Transcription key

(0.5)	a pause in tenths of seconds
(.)	a pause of less than two tenths of a second
=	latching between utterances
[	overlapping talk
..hh/hh..	in-breath/out-breath
y(hh)es	'bubbling through laughter'
:	stretched sound
↑↓	rising or falling intonation
a:	less marked falls in pitch
a:	less marked rises in pitch
° °	noticeably quieter
< >	noticeably slower

Police caution transcript using conversation analysis, adapted from 'Extract 18: Heard it all before' (Carter, 2013):

45 P1→	and the la:st thing >which is very important is that you don't have to say anything
46	unless you wish to but anything you do say may be given in evide:nce do you
47	understand th↓at<=
48	=yeah
49	(0.2)
50 P1	r↓ight (.)

Who should do the transcription?

Well, the first answer you might expect us to write is YOU! Of course, the person best placed to do a transcription is the person who conducted the interview. As the primary researcher, you will have the recollection of the emotional responses, body language clues and, most importantly, you might be able to remember key words which are perhaps hard to hear in a recording. Moreover, transcription involves a re-immersion back into the original context of the interview encounter, which can be important for shaping your analysis. You should keep your reflexive journal close to hand to remind yourself of important contextual information as you are transcribing. It is also helpful to have your interview summaries (we recommended you prepared these in Chapter 7) open alongside your transcription so you can add to this file (for example, including a few notable quotations) to aid you when you start your analysis.

Careful transcription takes a long time to complete and we do understand that when you are under enormous time pressures, you need to find short cuts. On average, for a competent typist, it will take around six hours per recorded hour of time to transcribe. This can be longer if your participant speaks fast or is difficult to understand. You can do the maths – how many hours will it take you to transcribe *your* recorded data?

We understand that doing your own transcription may not always be feasible. If you are a student with an assignment to complete, bear in mind that unless your assessment specifically asks you to transcribe something yourself, then it is not usually against assessment rules to pay for transcription to be done by an external agency. In fact, most experienced researchers pay for transcription to be done externally when working on large research contracts. (Do check first with your module leader/supervisor that you are allowed to employ a transcriber.)

Case study 10.1

A lesson in giving clear instructions to a transcription service

When conducting research for her PhD, Bethany had fully intended to complete the transcription process on her own. She believed that a full immersion and reflexive engagement with her data as she transcribed would greatly benefit the analysis, given her psychosocial approach. However, a family tragedy during this period meant that her time became increasingly pressured and she was limited as to what was realistically possible. She had to finish her thesis one way or another, so the plan to transcribe her own data was relinquished in favour of completing her PhD on time.

By the point of the tragedy, she had fully transcribed a few of her own interviews, but the rest she paid to have transcribed by various friends or friends of friends who could get the work done quickly and cheaply. She did not consider providing the transcribers with any instructions or templates – she just wanted the words typed so she could use them as quickly as possible. The resulting data was usable for her doctoral research, and it was not particularly problematic for her as she was familiar with the interviews. Where there were gaps in the transcription, she could listen back to the audio for clarification. She knew what to anonymise and who was who amongst her participants. As an immediate resource for her PhD, this data was OK. However, the transcripts really needed to be formatted in a much clearer way if she wanted to share or archive them for future use. (Five years later, she retrospectively processed all her data to archival standards for depositing in the UK Data Archive.)

Not surprisingly, the transcribers, without clear instructions from Bethany, all produced very different quality transcripts. One transcriber, for instance, transcribed every reassuring 'hmm' and 'umm' noise she made as an interviewer as a separate turn-take, thus making the transcript around 50 pages longer than it needed to be. Some did not add speaker tags (which indicate who is speaking). There were spelling mistakes, dates written as text instead of numbers, some parts anonymised and others not, and in some cases, text that was missed out because it was inaudible or considered irrelevant. File names were inconsistent, and there were either no headers or headers with ambiguous information in them at the start of the transcripts. The fonts were also inconsistent, and often the transcripts had no page numbering. Then, most concerning of all was when a transcriber's husband approached Bethany to tell her about how interesting her research was and that he had enjoyed reading the interviews! She had not considered that confidentiality agreements needed to extend to those involved in the processing of the data as well.

Question

1. What lessons can you learn from this example?
2. What would you do differently?

Right from the start of your research process, it is important that you have clarity on the style and format you require for the transcriptions. If you pay for an external transcriber then be clear about your expectations of the quality of the transcript, choose a reputable transcription service (maybe seek advice from your tutor) and have a written agreement on the price in advance. Transcribers will usually charge by the audio-recorded minute rather than by how long it takes them to do it. You should give the transcriber a list of instructions on how you would like your transcripts to be formatted.

Transcription processes

Transcription can be a time-consuming and frustrating process, however there are some software packages and technical equipment which can make the process much easier.

Software packages such as Dragon and NVivo can do a lot of the hard work for you. Dragon trains to a singular voice and is not ideal for multiple speakers in an interview. NVivo allows you to upload an audio file and automatically transcribes it for you. This is an additional, paid-for service, which accompanies NVivo 12, and you must purchase pay-as-you-go credits which give you minutes of transcription time. This automated, cloud-based transcription service claims to have a 90% accuracy rate, and when Katy and I have used this, we have found it to be useful and quite reliable.

If you are conducting your interviews via a video-conferencing platform such as Zoom, there is an automated transcription process built in. However, this automatic service is often quite unreliable. The transcripts these platforms create are often full of errors because when people speak quickly or with a strong accent, the computer cannot recognise all the words. You need to carefully check and edit any transcript prepared by an online service or third party. With automated transcripts, it is important to check the speaker tags, edit any inaccuracies and take out any unnecessary extraneous chat which might have been captured, and decisions about what to keep and what to omit continue to remain crucial.

If you need to do the interview transcription yourself, rather than paying for an automated or professional service, then you can ease the process with the use of a transcription foot pedal. This is a useful tool for keeping your hands focused on your typing, whilst using the foot pedal to control pause, rewind and fast-forward on the audio. Software such as NCH Express Scribe is a pedal-controlled digital transcription audio player which we find particularly useful. You can link your foot pedal, set your controls, upload your audio files, transcribe your data and export your completed files from this software. This software, along with NVivo Transcription, also allows you to slow down or speed up the recording, which can make the process much easier. Keyboard functions such as F4 (Stop), F7 (Rewind), F8 (Fast Forward) and F9 (Play) (http://help.nchsoftware.com/help/en/scribe/win/keys.html) are also useful short cuts if you don't have a foot pedal. Finally, the other key piece of equipment is a pair of good quality headphones, which can help keep you focused, and enables you to listen very carefully and more accurately to the recording.

Transcription templates

In Box 10.3, you will see an example of how the interview with {Penny} was first transcribed by an inexperienced transcriber who Bethany paid to transcribe the interview quickly and cheaply. You will then see how this was transformed into an archival standard.

Box 10.3

Transcription transformation

File was labelled [Interview_2_with_Penny [1][1]]

Interview with Penny

Interview 2

In her office

6th November 2007

The first set of questions is about aging mostly and the experiences of aging. Um first of all, if you could tell me your date of birth?

Fifteenth of the fifth forty eight

Ok could you start by describing yourself and telling me a few words about yourself

About myself, oh my god, I'm 55 and the mother of 3 daughters, Lisa, Mandy, and Nicola, um I therefore die my hair constantly, I have still got one daughter still living at home and I am happily married. I have been married for 31 years, I know I don't seem like it [said in a breathy jokey voice].

Mmm

I was a late mother, I didn't have children til I was 30 and we were married for 6 years and I just didn't want to be a mother, but then again I didn't want to get married, so, and then all of a sudden I wanted it like yesterday. I work everyday,......but not full time at the moment and I am very happy with my lot.

Sorry how old did you say you were? {coughs}

55, botox is a wonderful thing

{Clears throat}

Commented [A1]: The original file was labelled like this. This is poor version control. What does the [1][1] stand for? Might be better as Int.001_final.

Commented [A2]: Might an iD be useful too?

Commented [A3]: Is this the second interview with this particular respondent or the second interview in the study as a whole?

Commented [A4]: More contextual information might be beneficial

Commented [A5]: Do you want these "Ums" in here?

Commented [A6]: It would be easier to read dates if they were written numerically. It would also make it easier to search for dates in a transcript if written numerically.

Commented [A7]: There are no line breaks here

Commented [A8]: Clear speech demarcation and speaker tags are crucial in transcripts. They are not used here.

Commented [A9]: Are these pseudonyms? How can you be sure?

At what point should pseudonyms be added? If they are repeat interviews as these interviews were then it might be best to do it after fieldwork is completed.

Commented [A10]: Check spelling

Commented [A11]: How much description of intonation should be included and what are the rules for assigning it?

Commented [A12]: Are all sounds like 'mmm's going to be represented?

These 'mmms' have been put into the turn taking sequence which makes the transcript overly long (by 50 pages!).

Commented [A13]: What do these ellipses mean?

Commented [A14]: Do you want to include all these extraneous noises?

Commented [A15]: Page number needed

Commented [A16]: Do you want square or round brackets when noting extraneous sounds?

Figure 10.1 Penny's interview extract, transcribed by an inexperienced transcriber

Pseudonym: Penny

Number of interviews in transcript: 2

Date of interview: 2007

Location: Her home

Gender: Female

Age: 55

(Continued)

Figure 10.2 (Continued)

Marital status: Married

Children: 3 girls in their 20s – all have left home at one stage, but the middle daughter has now returned

Parents: Mum died a few years ago; Dad lives independently but needs some care

Grandchildren: None

Class Category (based on HoH): C2

Bethany: **The first set of questions is about ageing mostly and the experiences of ageing. First of all, if you could tell me your date of birth?**

Penny: 15th of the 5th, 1948.

Bethany: **OK, could you start by describing yourself and telling me a few words about yourself?**

Penny: About myself, oh my god, I'm 55 and the mother of 3 daughters, {Lindy}, {Emma} and {Lucy}, um I therefore dye my hair constantly, I have still got one daughter still living at home and I am happily married. I have been married for 31 years; I know I don't seem like it [said in a breathy jokey voice]. I was a late mother, I didn't have children 'til I was 30 and we were married for 6 years and I just didn't want to be a mother, but then again I didn't want to get married, so, and then all of a sudden I wanted it like yesterday. I work every day, but not full time at the moment and I am very happy with my lot.

Bethany: **Sorry how old did you say you were?**

Penny: 55. Botox is a wonderful thing

Figure 10.2 Penny's interview extract, transcribed to archival standard

Storing your transcripts

At the time of writing, most researchers record their audio data on digital recorders, saving digital files to their computers, or they are using video-conferencing platforms and saving the files to cloud storage. However, it was not that many years ago that researchers were recording on cassette tapes, and reel-to-reel tapes before that, both of which have since become obsolete. When we started our research careers, data files were stored on floppy disks, but now very few computers can use a floppy disk and even USB flash drives are going out of fashion. Technology moves fast so it is important that you store your digital data in a way that you can access in 10+ years' time. If you are not sure your digital data can stand the test of time, then you should have a plan to review how your data is stored and to review this every year or so.

Any hard-copy data you have should always be stored securely, with any confidential information, in a locked filing cabinet. If you are planning to keep documents long term, it would be good practice to digitise these and have them as securely kept computer files.

You need to ask yourself this question: 'If I were to return to these files in 10 years' time, would I still be able to understand what was in them?'

Activity 10.2

File naming

Compare these file names. Which one are you most likely to understand in 10 years' time?

232020InterviewP2.2.20.final.bmb.house1_final.doc
Interview1of2_Penny_02.03.2020.doc
Int001_1of2_02032020.doc
02032020_Int001_1of2

Questions

1. What information should you include in your file name?
2. How will you understand it in 10 years' time?
3. How can you ensure that it remains consistent throughout your research project?
4. Have a look at your own system for file storage on your computer. How might you improve your file naming? How might you improve your folder structure?

Summary

It is good practice to be able to share your data with others, not least your examiners or supervisor should you be asked to evidence your research practice. And if you intend to continue with a research career, it is worth noting that many research funding councils now require qualitative data transcripts to be deposited with an archive as a condition of funding. It is therefore important that you are open and transparent about your research procedures and that your data transcripts are easily shareable. High-quality, consistent transcription, and appropriate storage of your data (along with solid anonymisation and permission to share your data; see Chapter 5), are essential if sharing is to be made possible.

Top tip summary

This time, we provide a slightly more detailed set of top tips, which combines data management tips from this chapter with ethical advice from Chapter 5:

- Be prepared to share your data. Research funders and journal publishers are increasingly expecting research data to be open, transparent and shared. To share data, you need to develop robust procedures to process and store your research data so that it is useable in the future.
- Integrate data management into your research plan. Research data management should be an integral part of the research process, considered and planned from the start, and reviewed throughout the life cycle of the project.
- Remember that documenting your data is important. Think about whether someone in 10 years' time could read through your data collection and understand it. What else might they need to know about it? Are all your research processes adequately documented?
- Follow a standard transcription template. This is important whether you are doing your own transcription or whether you are paying a transcription service to do it. If you are working in a team, everyone should be transcribing in the same way for the whole project. How you transcribe your data depends very much on your theoretical and methodological approach, so these are decisions you will have to make (see Corti et al., 2014: 63–6).
- Ask transcribers to sign a confidentiality agreement. Transcribers are often privy to confidential information, and it is important to ask them to sign a confidentiality agreement, so that they too protect the data they have access to. We ask our transcribers to return a signed hard copy or an electronically signed digital copy of that agreement before commencing their work.
- Plan for the costs of data management. Transcription can be expensive, so make sure, if you are planning to use a professional transcription service, that you have factored in that cost. Agree a rate of pay with a transcription service in advance. Intelligent verbatim transcription may be cheaper than full verbatim transcription as it is less time-consuming, so ask the service about this option.
- Ensure consent forms and information sheets include permission to share. It is important that consent forms ask participants to share their data beyond the use of the original research project. You may need to use their data in many different, and often unexpected, ways. Might you use your data in future teaching? News articles? Might you archive your data? You can use a 'catch all' phrase such as 'Your data will be used in this research project and may also be used in future research and teaching activities.'
- When anonymising, keep maximum meaningful information. Make sure that clear identifying information, such as names, are changed to appropriate pseudonyms and that indirect identifiers are meaningfully changed. But

beware of over-anonymisation as this can lead to a loss in data quality and authenticity.

- Do not assume that all participants want to be anonymous. We offer participants a choice on their consent form as to whether they would like their real name used or not. If they choose to remain anonymous, then they also get a choice of what they would like their name changed to. We see this as an empowering choice for participants. If someone chooses to use their real name, we double-check after the interview that they are still happy with the data they have divulged. We also make them aware of any potential consequences of having their real name used.

- Digitise and store your data, so that it is secure and accessible in the future. Data, if stored on non-proprietary software or on particular media such as a cassette or USB, can become useless if that technology becomes obsolete. Review how your data is stored and consider whether its storage conditions need to change with changes in technology. Also think about how your work is file-named. Would you be able to understand what each file contains, just by its file name, in 10 years' time?

11

PREPARE YOUR NEXT STEPS

Learning objectives

On completing this chapter, you should be able to:

- Recognise the key role of a reflexive journal
- Understand the basic principles of thematic analysis
- Devise a strategy for your next steps
- Identify sources to help you analyse and write up your interview data.

You've done the interview, recorded your reflections and have your transcription ready. Now, it is time to start your analysis. Though there is a phase dedicated to analysis in any project, your analysis actually started much earlier on in the process. From the moment you formulated your research question, designed your interview guide and began writing your reflexive journal, you have been formulating your own ideas about what is going on and what the data collected might mean – these were the first stages of your analysis. The systematic exploration of your interview data at the stage of analysis is the continuation of an ongoing process.

This chapter reviews your progress so far and points you in the direction of how to start analysing your data. We revisit the reflexive journal you started at the beginning of this book and should have been adding to throughout your data collection. This is a vital tool to aid analysis. We do not cover data analysis in depth because the approach you take will be dependent on your academic discipline and the conventions of different types of analyses. Within the space constraints of this final chapter, we instead very briefly outline how to undertake a thematic analysis (which is arguably the most common mode of qualitative data analysis) and point you in the direction of further sources to consult. We also offer some introductory guidance on writing up your interviews.

How what you have learnt so far connects to data analysis

When you started this book, you considered why you wanted to use interviews in your research project, and we discussed the nature of the knowledge created through this method. You might remember that there is a debate about how far interview data reflects the interviewee's reality *beyond* the interview and how far it is constructed between interviewee and interviewer *within* the interview. We recommended taking a pragmatic position between these two poles, and suggested keeping a reflexive journal to track how any assumptions, interactions and research choices may have influenced data collection. These reflexive notes are important, regardless of the approach to data analysis you take.

Throughout the book, you have learnt about some of the different varieties of qualitative interview, but we have mostly focused on how to do semi-structured interviews (though most of the advice on recruitment, ethics and managing interview relationships is applicable to other styles of qualitative interviewing). The semi-structured interview is characterised by the interview guide (which captures what the researcher wants to find out) and follow-up questions, probes and prompts (which allow for topics relevant to your participant to also be explored). Your thoughts on the creation of the guide, your reflections on how this guide worked in practice and any other relevant insights into the way you interacted with your participants within the interview, should have been captured in your reflexive journal.

This reflexive journal is vital when you come to the stage of analysis. It will allow you to contextualise your interview data with relevant information – such as whether the way you phrased a question had an influence on how your participant responded, or whether the rapport (or lack of it) between interviewee and interviewer led to insights being truthfully shared, or the role that identities played in shaping what could and could not be said.

Box 11.1

Stop & Reflect

The reflexive journal

Besides being a tool of ongoing reflection for your analysis, can you think of any other reasons why we have emphasised the importance of keeping a reflexive journal throughout this book?

You might have thought about how a reflexive journal can act as an audit trail to record how decisions were made and to document any challenges or issues that arose in relation to the study's aim, design and methods. Having a reflexive journal is one way you can demonstrate the credibility of your research.

Patton (2002) points out that, whilst in quantitative research discussions of credibility (sometimes referred to as validity and reliability) relate to the construction and use of standardised measures or instruments, in qualitative research it is the researcher who is the 'instrument'. Therefore, credibility in qualitative research 'hinges to a great extent on the skill, competence, and rigor' of the researcher (Patton, 2002: 14). Meticulous record keeping through a reflexive journal is an important practice that not only helps you develop as a researcher and become more familiar with the data you collect, but opens up the possibility for others to audit the consistency of your research (see Noble and Smith, 2015).

In addition to the reflexive journal, we encouraged you to make summaries of the content of your interviews and add to these at the transcription stage (see Chapters 7 and 10). If you did not manage to do this, we would recommend you take some time now to complete this exercise. Your summaries can include a few notable quotations from each participant, and this will really help the analytic process.

Activity 11.1

Reviewing your journal and summaries

Before you start on the phase of data analysis, you should carefully read through your reflexive journal and interview summaries. Do this now and make yourself a few notes about recurring ideas, points to look out for and your hunches about what this might mean for your research question.

Analysing your interviews

The fundamental feature of any qualitative data analysis is writing about your data – whether this is summarising key themes or patterns that emerge or developing your analytic ideas. Whichever approach to data analysis you take, remember that writing is a 'method of discovery' (Barbour, 2014: 313). Most forms of qualitative analysis also involve some form of coding or labelling of the text for key themes, concepts or ideas.

Table 11.1 outlines two broad traditions of qualitative data analysis. The approach you adopt relates to your understanding of the nature of knowledge construction within and beyond the interview – or to epistemological and ontological assumptions (see Chapter 1).

Table 11.1 Two broad approaches to analysing qualitative interview data (adapted from Spencer et al., 2014b: 272)

Type of approach	Key features	Examples
'Substantive'	• Data treated as window into participant's social world, 'representing feelings, perceptions and events that exist' *beyond* the data • Focus on what the text *says*	Thematic analysis Grounded theory
'Structural' or 'Constructionist'	• Data is the phenomenon under study; analysts are interested in language and the construction of talk, text and interaction *within* the interview • Focus on what the text *does*	Narrative analysis Discourse analysis

A brief introduction to thematic analysis

Thematic analysis is probably the most commonly used method for analysing qualitative interview data (Braun and Clarke, 2006, 2013; King et al., 2019; Rubin and Rubin, 2012; Spencer et al., 2014b). Put simply, this approach involves systematically and closely reading all your data to find and label the recurring and distinctive features of your participants' accounts, sometimes referred to as themes. Box 11.2 offers a useful analogy for thinking about what thematic analysis involves, and Box 11.3 summarises what counts as a 'theme' when analysing qualitative interview data.

Box 11.2

A helpful analogy for thematic coding

We often use the analogy of moving boxes to help describe what it is you are trying to do when you are coding your data for key themes.

If you were moving to a new house, you might start packing up your belongings in boxes labelled 'bathroom', 'bedroom', 'lounge', for instance. However, you might find there is too much stuff in your 'lounge' box, and you want to break down the contents of this box into different boxes, labelled 'books', 'DVDs', 'ornaments', and so on. The labels you put on the boxes have consequences for how you will unpack them at the other end – for example, the order you unpack them and the location you put them in. You might have a clear idea as you start the process of boxing up your stuff how you want to label the boxes, or you might decide the labels as you go. As you go through the process, some of the labels you thought you would need turn out not to be very useful; some of your stuff does not fit obviously with the label but you decide to put your item in there anyway and make a note to yourself; and you discover new things at the bottom of your old drawers that warrant a label of their own.

And we could continue, substituting 'labels' for 'themes' and 'boxes of belongings' for 'your interview data', but we hope you get the gist of what we are saying here. Applying themes to your data is an active process and there are always alternative ways of coding your data depending on your research focus. How you conduct this task will have consequences for your ongoing analysis and for what you can say with your data.

Box 11.3

What counts as a theme?

The following criteria (taken from King et al., 2019: 200) detail what counts as a 'theme':

1. Defining a theme 'involves the researcher in making choices about what to include, what to discard, and how to interpret participants' words'
2. 'The term "theme" implies some degree of repetition' (something mentioned once cannot be classed as a theme but might still be important in your analysis)
3. 'Themes must be distinct from one another' – although there may be some overlap between themes, they will not be useful for your analysis if you cannot distinguish them in your interpretations.

When it comes to the process of doing a thematic analysis, Table 11.2 offers a quick glance overview of the key steps involved. You will notice that analysis begins with you familiarising yourself with your data and good data management (things we have stressed throughout the book). It then involves systematically reading all your interview data to develop a coding frame which captures the distinctive and recurring features. This coding frame is then applied to the interview data, usually with the help of a qualitative software package (see below). In the final stage, you review your coded segments, alongside any notes you have been making throughout the process, and try to make sense of them. You might summarise each theme and generate descriptions and typologies to capture similarities and differences across your sample. At the final stage, you will be trying to offer explanations and applications to theory in relation to your research question.

Table 11.2 Key steps of thematic analysis

Key stage	What is involved
Data management and familiarisation	• Transcribe your data fully and capture your initial thoughts as memos. If using Word to transcribe, you can use the comment function, or if you're using CAQDAS, you can use the memo function • Organise your data into relevant files and folders – although this is a practical task, you will be making choices about how to group your data • Make summaries of your interviews, drawing out notable quotes • Re-read all your transcripts for key points in relation to your key question (you can do this line by line if you choose)
Coding your data	• Review the key points you have listed above and try to group them loosely by topic/theme, keeping in mind your research aims • Develop a coding frame using these loose groupings • Test out your coding frame on 2–3 transcripts and make any revisions to your coding frame (add or remove codes as appropriate) • Systematically apply the coding frame to all your interview data • Don't forget to keep taking memos of your ideas as you go along
Developing analytical ideas	• Look at coded segments by theme and revisit your memos so you can write summaries of each theme • Remember to look across cases and within cases (e.g. what different interviewees say about your themes, as well as how each interviewee talks about this theme throughout their interview) • Make note of any patterns you spot and develop categories or typologies to group similar responses • Connect and apply your data to theoretical ideas and develop explanations for what you have found

Using computers to help

Before the invention of Computer Assisted Qualitative Data Analysis Software (CAQDAS), researchers literally used to cut up their interview transcripts and sort them physically into piles, folders and boxes. The process is made a lot easier with software such as MAXQDA (Katy and Bethany's preferred package), NVivo and ATLAS.ti. There are many advantages to using these programs (see Table 11.3), especially when you have a lot of data to manage. The core feature of these packages is the 'code and retrieve' function – you can tag sections of your interview according to your themes, and then retrieve these tagged segments on their own to explore the variation of responses.

We recommend using a computer program if you have lots of interview data, but the process can be managed by hand, using highlighters and scissors. Many undergraduate projects involve only a small number of interviews and you will need to decide whether the investment in time in learning how to use the program is worth it. For us, the most important part about coding your data is to engage with the process actively. If you are mindlessly tagging/highlighting data for hours and have not written any comments to yourself about this process, you are doing it wrong! Analysis should be an active process and you should be reflecting on and writing about the many judgements you are making along the way. Computers will not do the analysis for you, but they can aid the process.

Table 11.3 Advantages and disadvantages of using CAQDAS packages

Advantages	Disadvantages
• Saves time once you know how to use CAQDAS	• Can take time to learn how to use CAQDAS
• Closeness to your data (all files, codes and retrieved segments in one window)	• Expensive to purchase (though most universities do subscribe to one package, and software companies offer discounts for students)
• Ease of 'code and retrieve'	• They don't do the analysis for you
• Allows you to keep memos and comments on your analytical thinking	• They can take your data out of context by technologically distancing you from it (see the psycho-social critique of CAQDAS)
• You can explore your data using keyword searches and create automatic codes	• They promote a particular way of doing analysis (e.g. code and retrieve)
• Visual tools and statistical functions can help you explore relationships between codes (but be careful how you use them)	• There is a risk of interpreting frequency of codes as indicative of their meaning
• Some packages (like MAXQDA) allow you to export a report which is pre-populated with your retrieved segments by theme	
• You can work together as a team using cloud-based services	

Some suggestions for further reading on data analysis

In this section, we offer some suggestions for further reading on qualitative data analysis and organise these according to the type of analysis you intend to undertake. If you want to find a broader introductory overview to these different types of analysis within one or two texts, we would recommend:

- Brinkmann S and Kvale S (2015) *InterViews: Learning the Craft of Qualitative Research Interviewing* (3rd edition). London: SAGE.
- King N, Horrocks C and Brooks J (2019) *Interviews in Qualitative Research* (2nd edition). London: SAGE.

Thematic analysis

Though this chapter has given you a brief introduction to thematic analysis, we would strongly recommend reading more widely on how to do this. Braun and Clarke's (2006) paper on thematic analysis in psychology is widely cited but their textbook includes even more detail on how to undertake this style of qualitative analysis. The two chapters by Spencer et al. (2014a, b) in an edited collection written by Natcen researchers, also provide a comprehensive overview of how to undertake a thematic analysis.

- Braun V and Clarke V (2013) *Successful Qualitative Research: A Practical Guide for Beginners*. London: SAGE.
- Spencer L et al. (2014) 'Analysis: Principles and processes' and 'Analysis in practice'. In: Ritchie J, Lewis J, McNaughton Nicholls C, et al. (eds) *Qualitative Research Practice* (2nd edition). Los Angeles, CA: SAGE, pp. 269–345.

Grounded theory

Grounded theory is associated with the generation of theory from qualitative data, but it is not usually an approach to begin exploring at the point of analysis. Whilst many qualitative researchers claim to have taken a grounded theory approach, in our experience very few follow the principles of iterative data collection and coding. Charmaz's (2014) book offers a comprehensive introduction to this approach, including where the method originated from, some of the discrepancies between different grounded theory approaches, and how to apply these principles in qualitative research projects:

- Charmaz K (2014) *Constructing Grounded Theory: A Practical Guide through Qualitative Analysis* (2nd edition). London: SAGE.

Narrative analysis

There are different approaches to narrative analysis, but a good introduction is offered by Gibbs (2007), who describes the key features to look out for within narrative interviews, and Riessman (2008), who details how to approach a narrative analysis in different ways. If you have undertaken free association narrative interviews, Hollway and Jefferson (2013) offer important guidance about using reflexive interpretations to guide the analysis and advise against using computer packages to assist you:

- Gibbs G (2007) *Analyzing Qualitative Data*. London: SAGE.
- Hollway W and Jefferson T (2013) *Doing Qualitative Research Differently* (2nd edition). London: SAGE.
- Riessman CK (2008) *Narrative Methods for the Human Sciences*. London: SAGE.

Discourse analysis

Discourse analysis is interested in how people use language and cultural repertoires to construct their social and psychological realities. The focus of analysis is on how people put discourses to work and how these are often used in contradictory or fragmented ways within people's narratives. Potter and Wetherell's (1987) foundational text remains a must-read for those contemplating a discourse analysis, whilst Willig's (2014) chapter offers a useful introduction to the field:

- Potter J and Wetherell M (1987) *Discourse and Social Psychology: Beyond Attitudes and Behaviour*. London: Sage.
- Willig C (2014) Discourses and discourse analysis. In: Flick U (ed.) *The SAGE Handbook of Qualitative Data Analysis*. London: SAGE, pp. 341–53.

Writing up your interviews

When it comes to writing up your interviews, the best place to start is by re-visiting the memos/journal entries you made to yourself throughout the analysis process, and your summaries of key themes (if you undertook a thematic analysis). Your notes will reveal the beginnings of your key findings, and your summaries of key themes will help ensure your reporting is grounded in the words and experiences of your interviewees.

Writing up your qualitative analysis is a challenging but creative process. It is a good idea to start writing early because 'writing is thinking' (Wolcott, 2009: 22). Establish a routine for writing – this might be at a set time of the day in a quiet space free from distractions (especially social media and emails). Some of our students have found it helpful to set themselves a word limit for each day (maybe 500 or 750 words). Even if all those words do not end up in the report – 'the precondition for writing well is being able to write badly and to write when you are not in the mood' (Elbow, cited in Wolcott, 2009: 45).

When crafting your essay/dissertation/research report, it is important to display your authorial voice. Be clear about what your argument is and use qualitative data (quotations from your participants) to support your findings. Many students ask whether they can write their qualitative projects in the first person. It is always a good idea to check with your module supervisor, but it is common practice for qualitative researchers to write in the first person. After all, you have collected the data and it is your interpretation you are reporting so it makes more sense to say 'I' rather than 'the researcher'.

Your reflexive journal will be your best friend when you are writing up your research. You should provide a clear account of the methods used, details on sampling, how the data was gathered, and note any challenges or important insights that impact on the interpretation of the data – all the things you should have been recording in your journal throughout your research.

Box 11.4

Stop & Reflect

Why do you think you should include quotations from your interviews within your assignment/dissertation/research project?

There are a number of reasons why, the main one being that you have spent a lot of time and effort gathering this data from participants who have experiences that are relevant to your research question, so it makes sense to use their words in your analysis. Others you might have thought of are:

- To allow 'the reader to judge the "fit" between your data and your understandings and interpretations of them' (Braun and Clarke, 2013: 251)
- To offer evidence for your claims
- To give participants a voice – demonstrate the type of language they use and the meanings they attach to the phenomena under study

- To display the diversity of experiences across your sample
- To illustrate a key point or theme
- To enhance readability.

Probably one of the things that students struggle the most with is how to use quotations from their interviews effectively. Table 11.4 offers our key do's and don'ts when it comes to using quotations in your writing. Another common error students often make when writing up qualitative research is using numeric or quasi-numeric (i.e. 'many people think', 'a few people said', 'some interviewees reported') statements. This is misleading because qualitative samples are purposively selected and do not allow for statistical inference (see Chapter 4). Some suggestions of how to avoid this are to try to present a range of responses and, if recurrence of opinion/experience does occur, explain why (see White et al., 2014 for more guidance on this point).

Table 11.4 Do's and don'ts when using quotations from your interviews

Do	Don't
• Humanise participants by assigning their words to a name (pseudonym) rather than a letter or number	• Use the same quotation more than once in your report
• Display diversity – we would be suspicious of a qualitative report that suggests everyone agreed or shared the same perspective; there are always nuances and contradictions to be highlighted	• Leave your quotations to speak for themselves; you should introduce and interpret any quotation you include
• Indent quotations longer than 40 words	• Compromise the confidentiality and anonymity you promised your participants
• Save words by editing quotations down, using [...] to indicate you've done this	• Over-quote – too many quotations make it difficult for the reader to follow

There are lots of good resources to help with writing up qualitative research (Braun and Clarke, 2013; White et al., 2014; Wolcott, 2009), but probably the most important advice we can offer is to read lots of published qualitative research because there is so much to learn from how others have done this.

A note to finish

You have reached the end of this book and we hope you have found it a practical and helpful guide for planning and conducting qualitative interviews for your university assignments, dissertations, PhDs and research projects. From both of us

(Bethany and Katy), we want to wish you the best of luck as you move on to the exciting phase of analysing and writing up your data.

Top tip summary

- Keep your reflexive journal updated throughout your research project, including during the analysis and writing-up phase.
- Follow up on some of the suggested readings in this chapter before starting your analysis.
- Whichever approach to analysis you take, ensure you are writing about the process and make notes about your initial interpretations of the data.
- Use your notes and reflexive journal to guide the writing-up process.
- Use quotations from your interviews appropriately in your research reports/ assignments (use Box 11.4 and Table 11.4 to help you with this).

REFERENCES

Alderson P (2019) Education, conflict, peace-building and critical realism. *Education and Conflict Review*, 2: 55–8.

Arthur S, Mitchell M, Lewis J, et al. (2014) Designing fieldwork. In: Ritchie J, Lewis J, McNaughton Nicholls C, et al. (eds) *Qualitative Research Practice*. London: SAGE, pp. 147–76.

Atkinson P and Silverman D (1997) Kundera's immortality: The interview society and the invention of the self. *Qualitative Inquiry*, 3(3): 304–25.

Atkinson R (1998) *The Life Story Interview*. London: SAGE.

Aurini J, Heath M and Howells S (2016) *The How To of Qualitative Research*. London: SAGE.

Barbour R (2014) *Introducing Qualitative Research: A Student's Guide* (2nd edition). London: SAGE.

Bloor M, Frankland J, Thomas M, et al. (2001) *Focus Groups in Social Research*. London: SAGE.

Bott E (2010) Favourites and others: Reflexivity and the shaping of subjectivities and data in qualitative research. *Qualitative Research*, 10(2): 159–73.

Bourke B (2014) Positionality: Reflecting on the research process. *The Qualitative Report*, 19(33): 1–9.

Braun V and Clarke V (2006) Using thematic analysis in psychology. *Qualitative Research in Psychology*, 3(2): 77–101.

Braun V and Clarke V (2013) *Successful Qualitative Research: A Practical Guide for Beginners*. London: SAGE.

Brinkmann S (2018) The interview. In: Denzin N and Lincoln Y (eds) *The SAGE Handbook of Qualitative Research* (5th edition). Los Angeles, CA: SAGE.

Brinkmann S and Kvale S (2015) *InterViews: Learning the Craft of Qualitative Research Interviewing* (3rd edition). London: SAGE.

Brown N and Leigh JS (2019) *Creativity and playfulness in higher education research* [Online paper]. Available at https://discovery.ucl.ac.uk/id/eprint/10058420/3/Brown_18%2002%2026%20Creativity%20and%20playfulness%20in%20HE%20research.pdf (accessed 26/4/21) pp. 1–20.

Buse C and Twigg J (2013) Dress, dementia and the embodiment of identity. *Dementia*, 12(3): 326–36.

Buse C and Twigg J (2015) Clothing, embodied identity and dementia: Maintaining the self through dress. *Age, Culture, Humanities*, 2: 71–96.

Cameron H (2005) Asking the tough questions: A guide to ethical practices in interviewing young children. *Early Child Development and Care*, 175(6): 597–610.

Carter E (2013) *Analysing Police Interviews: Laughter, Confessions and the Tape.* London: Bloomsbury.

Charmaz K (2014) *Constructing Grounded Theory: A Practical Guide through Qualitative Analysis* (2nd edition). London: SAGE.

Clarke N, Barnett C, Cloke P, et al. (2007a) Globalising the consumer: Doing politics in an ethical register. *Political Geography*, 26(3): 231–49.

Clarke N, Barnett C, Cloke P, et al. (2007b) The political rationalities of fair-trade consumption in the United Kingdom. *Politics and Society*, 35(4): 583–607.

Corti L, Van den Eynden V, Bishop L and Woollard M (2014) *Managing and Sharing Research Data: A Guide to Good Practice.* London: SAGE.

Creswell J (2013) *Research Design: Qualitative, Quantitative and Mixed Methods Approaches.* London: SAGE.

Darbyshire P (2000) Guest editorial: From research on children to research with children. *Neonatal, Paediatric and Child Health Nursing*, 3(1): 2–3.

Deakin H and Wakefield K (2014) Skype interviewing: Reflections of two PhD researchers. *Qualitative Research*, 14(5): 603–16.

Denzin N and Lincoln Y (2018) *The SAGE Handbook of Qualitative Research* (5th edition). London: SAGE.

Dichter E (1960/2012) *The Strategy of Desire.* Oxon: Taylor & Francis.

Fargas Malet M, McSherry D, Larkin E and Robinson C (2010) Research with children: Methodological issues and innovative techniques. *Journal of Early Childhood Research*, 8(2): 175–92.

Finlay L (2002) Negotiating the swamp: The opportunity and challenge of reflexivity in research practice. *Qualitative Research*, 2(2): 209–30.

Fletcher, J (1966/1997) *The Situation Ethics: The New Morality* (2nd revised edition). London: John Knox Press.

Flick U (2014) *An Introduction to Qualitative Research* (5th edition). London: SAGE.

Frosh S and Baraitser L (2008) Psychoanalysis and psychosocial studies. *Psychoanalysis, Culture and Society.* London: Palgrave Macmillan, pp. 346–65.

Gibbs G (2007) *Analyzing Qualitative Data.* London: SAGE.

Goffman A (2014) *On the Run: Fugitive Life in an American City.* Chicago: University of Chicago Press.

Goffman E (1959) *The Presentation of Self in Everyday Life.* Harmondsworth: Penguin.

Gubrium J and Holstein J (2011) From the individual interview to the interview society. In: *Handbook of Interview Research.* London: SAGE, pp. 2–32.

Guest G, Bunce A and Johnson L (2006) How many interviews are enough? An experiment with data saturation and variability. *Field Methods*, 18(1): 59–82.

Hammersley M and Atkinson P (1995) *Ethnography: Principles in Practice* (2nd edition). London: Routledge.

Head E (2009) The ethics and implications of paying participants in qualitative research. *International Journal of Social Research Methodology*, 12(4): 335–44.

Hollway W and Jefferson T (2000) *Doing Qualitative Research Differently*. London: SAGE.

Hollway W and Jefferson T (2013) *Doing Qualitative Research Differently* (2nd edition). London: SAGE.

Holstein J and Gubrium J (2000) *The Self We Live By: Narrative Identity in a Post-modern World*. Oxford: Oxford University Press.

Holt A (2010) Using the telephone for narrative interviewing: A research note. *Qualitative Research*, 10(1): 113–21.

House ER (1990) An ethics of qualitative field studies. In: Guba EG (ed.) *The Paradigm Dialog*. Newbury Park, CA: SAGE, pp. 158–64.

Huisman K (2008) 'Does this mean you're not going to come visit me anymore?': An inquiry into an ethics of reciprocity and positionality in feminist ethnographic research. *Sociological Inquiry*, 78(3): 372–96.

Humphreys L (1970) *Tearoom Trade: Impersonal Sex in Public Places*. Chicago: Aldine.

Janghorban R, Roudsari RL and Taghipour A (2014) Skype interviewing: The new generation of online synchronous interview in qualitative research. *International Journal of Qualitative Studies on Health and Well-being*, 9(1): article 24152. [Online only]

Kegerreis S (2009) *Psychodynamic Counselling with Children and Young People*. London: Palgrave Macmillan.

Kellett M and Ding S (2004) Middle childhood. In: Fraser S, Lewis V, Ding S, Kellet M and Robinson C (eds) *Doing Research with Children and Young People*. London: Open University Press, pp. 161–74.

King N, Horrocks C and Brooks J (2019) *Interviews in Qualitative Research* (2nd edition). London: SAGE.

Kvale S (1996) *Interview Views: An Introduction to Qualitative Research Interviewing*. Thousand Oaks, CA: SAGE.

Kvale S and Brinkmann S (2009) *InterViews: Learning the Craft of Qualitative Research Interviewing* (2nd edition). London: SAGE.

Le Gallais (2008) 'Wherever I go there I am': Reflections on reflexivity and the research stance. *Reflective Practice: International and Multidisciplinary Perspectives*, 9(2): 145–55.

Lee RM (2008) Emory bogardus and the new social research. *Current Sociology*, 56(2): 307–21.

Letherby G (2003) *Feminist Research in Theory and Practice*. Buckingham: Open University Press.

Lincoln Y, Lynham S and Guba E (2018) Paradigmatic controversies, contradictions, and emerging confluences, revisited. In: *The SAGE Handbook of Qualitative Research* (5th edition). London: SAGE, pp. 108–50.

Lincoln YS and Guba EG (1986) But is it rigorous? Trustworthiness and authenticity in naturalistic evaluation. *New Directions for Program Evaluation*, 30: 73–84.

Lofland J, Snow D, Anderson L, et al. (2006) *Analysing Social Settings: A Guide to Qualitative Observation and Analysis*. Belmont, CA: Wadsworth.

Luff D (1999) Dialogue across the divides: 'Moments of rapport' and power in feminist research with anti-feminist women. *Sociology*, 33(4): 687–703.

Mason J (2002) *Qualitative Researching*. London: SAGE.

Maxwell JA (2004) Using qualitative methods for causal explanation. *Field Methods*, 16(3): 243–64.

Micheletti M (2010) *Political Virtue and Shopping*. Basingstoke: Palgrave Macmillan.

Milgram S (1974) *Obedience to Authority: An Experimental View*. New York: Harper & Row.

Miller J and Glassner B (2016) The 'inside' and the 'outside': Finding realities in interviews. In: Silverman D (ed.) *Qualitative Research* (4th edition). London: SAGE, pp. 51–66.

Morris A (2018) *A Practical Introduction to In-Depth Interviewing*. London: SAGE.

Noble, H and Smith, J (2015) Issues of validity and reliability in qualitative research, *Evidence-Based Nursing* 18: 34–35.

Oakley A (1981) Interviewing women: A contradiction in terms? In: Roberts H (ed.) *Doing Feminist Research*. London: Routledge & Kegan Paul, pp. 30–61.

O'Leary Z (2017) *The Essential Guide to Doing Your Research Project*. London: SAGE.

Patton MQ (2002) *Qualitative Research and Evaluation Methods* (3rd edition). London: SAGE.

Pawson R and Tilley N (1997) *Realistic Evaluation*. London: SAGE.

Pink S (2009) *Doing Sensory Ethnography*. London: SAGE.

Platt J (2011) The history of the interview. In: Gubrium J and Holstein J (eds) *Handbook of Interview Research*. London: SAGE, pp. 33–55.

Potter J and Wetherell M (1987) *Discourse and Social Psychology: Beyond Attitudes and Behaviour*. London: SAGE.

Punch K (2014) *Introduction to Social Research: Quantitative and Qualitative Approaches*. London: SAGE.

Riessman CK (2008) *Narrative Methods for the Human Sciences*. London: SAGE.

Ritchie J, Lewis J, Elam G, et al. (2014) Designing and selecting samples. In: Ritchie J, Lewis J, McNaughton Nicholls C, et al. (eds) *Qualitative Research Practice*. London: SAGE.

Rogers CR (1959/1989) A theory of therapy, personality, and interpersonal relationships as developed in the client-centered framework. In: Kirschenbaum H and Henderson V (eds) *The Carl Rogers Reader*. Boston: Houghton Mifflin.

Roper M (2003) Analysing the analysed: Transference and counter-transference in the oral history encounter. *Oral History*, 31(2): 20–32.

Roper M (2017) Subjectivities in the aftermath: Children of disabled soldiers after the Great War. In: Crouthamel J and Leese P (eds) *Psychological Trauma and the Legacies of the First World War*. London: Palgrave, pp. 165–91.

Roper M (2020) Little Ruby's hand: Daughters and the emotional economies of care in Britain after the Great War. In: Langhamer C, Noakes L and Siebrecht C (eds) *Total War: An Emotional History*. Proceedings of the British Academy, 227. Oxford: Oxford University Press.

Roseneil S (2006) The ambivalences of Angel's 'arrangement': A psychosocial lens on the contemporary condition of personal life. *The Sociological Review*, 54(4): 847–69.

Rosenhan DL (1973) On being sane in insane places. *Science*, 179: 250–8.

Rowe W (2014) Positionality. In: Coghlan D and Brydon-Miller M (eds) *The SAGE Encyclopaedia of Action Research*, Vol. 2. London: SAGE. p. 628.

Rubin H and Rubin I (2012) *Qualitative Interviewing: The Art of Hearing Data* (3rd edition). Thousand Oaks, CA: SAGE.

Ryan-Flood R and Gill R (eds) (2010) *Secrecy and Silence in the Research Process: Feminist Reflections*. London: Routledge.

Sacks H, Schegloff EA and Jefferson G (1974) A simplest systematics for the organization of turn taking for conversation. *Language*, 50(4): 696–735.

Salmons J (2012) *Cases in Online Interview Research*. Thousand Oaks, CA: SAGE.

Sharff C (2010) Silencing differences: The unspoken dimension of speaking for others. In: Ryan-Flood R and Gill R (eds) *Secrecy and Silence in the Research Process: Feminist Reflections*. London: Routledge, pp. 83–95.

Silva E, Warde A and Wright D (2009) Using mixed methods for analysing culture: The cultural capital and social exclusion project. *Cultural Sociology*, 3(2): 299–316.

Silverman D (2017) *Doing Qualitative Research* (5th edition). Los Angeles, CA: SAGE.

Smith KE (2006) Problematising power relations in 'elite' interviews. *Geoforum*, 37(4): 643–53.

Spencer L, Ritchie J, O'Conner W, et al. (2014a) Analysis in practice. In: Ritchie J, Lewis J, McNaughton Nicholls C, et al. (eds) *Qualitative Research Practice* (2nd edition). Los Angeles, CA: SAGE, pp. 295–345.

Spencer L, Ritchie J, Ormston R, et al. (2014b) Analysis: Principles and processes. In: Ritchie J, Lewis J, McNaughton Nicholls C, et al. (eds) *Qualitative Research Practice* (2nd edition). Los Angeles, CA: SAGE, pp. 269–93.

Stewart D, Shamdasani P and Rook D (2011) *Focus Groups*. Thousand Oaks, CA: SAGE.

Szmigin I, Carrigan M and McEachern MG (2009) The conscious consumer: Taking a flexible approach to ethical behaviour. *International Journal of Consumer Studies*, 33(2): 224–31.

Thomas, WI and Znaniecki, F (1918/1958). *The Polish Peasant in Europe and America*, 2 vols. New York: Dover.

Thompson P (1992) *The Edwardians: The Remaking of British Society*. London: Routledge.

Thwaites R (2017) (Re)examining the feminist interview: Rapport, gender 'matching', and emotional labour. *Frontiers in Sociology*, 2(18): 1–9.

Varul MZ (2009) Ethical selving in cultural contexts: Fairtrade consumption as an everyday ethical practice in the UK and Germany. *International Journal of Consumer Studies*, 33(2): 183–9.

Webb, B and Webb, S (1932) *Methods of Social Study*. London: Longmans Green.

Weller S (2017) Using internet video calls in qualitative (longitudinal) interviews: Some implications for rapport. *International Journal of Social Research Methodology*, 20(6): 613–25.

Wheeler K (2012) *Fair Trade and the Citizen-Consumer: Shopping for Justice*. Basingstoke: Palgrave Macmillan.

Wheeler K and Glucksmann M (2015) *Household Recycling and Consumption Work: Social and Moral Economies*. Basingstoke: Palgrave Macmillan.

White C, Woodfield K, Ritchie J, et al. (2014) Writing up qualitative research. In: Ritchie J, Lewis J, McNaughton Nicholls C, et al. (eds) *Qualitative Research Practice* (2nd edition). London: SAGE, pp. 367–400.

Willig C (2014) Discourses and discourse analysis. In: Flick U (ed.) *The SAGE Handbook of Qualitative Data Analysis*. London: SAGE, pp. 341–53.

Willis J and Todorov A (2006) First impressions: Making up your mind after a 100-ms exposure to a face. *Psychological Science*, 17(7): 592–8.

Willis R (2018) How Members of Parliament understand and respond to climate change. *The Sociological Review*, 66(3): 475–91.

Wolcott H (2009) *Writing Up Qualitative Research* (3rd edition). Thousand Oaks, CA: SAGE.

Yeo A, Legard R, Keegan J, et al. (2014) In-depth interviews. In: Ritchie J, Lewis J, McNaughton Nicholls C, et al. (eds) *Qualitative Research Practice* (2nd edition). Los Angeles, CA: SAGE, pp. 177–210.

Archived Collections

Morgan Brett B (2011) The negotiation of midlife: Exploring the subjective experience of ageing (PhD thesis). http://ethos.bl.uk/OrderDetails.do?did=1&uin=uk.bl.ethos.531545.

Morgan Brett B (2016) Negotiating midlife: Exploring the subjective experience of ageing, 2006–2008 [data collection]. UK Data Service, SN 8035, https://discover.ukdataservice.ac.uk/catalogue/?sn=8035.

Thompson P (2019) *Pioneers of Social Research, 1996–2012* [data collection] (4th edition). UK Data Service, SN 6226, http://doi.org/10.5255/UKDA-SN-6226-6.

Websites

British Association for Counselling and Psychotherapy (BACP) (February 2019) Ethical Guidelines for Research in the Counselling Professions – www.bacp.co.uk/events-and-resources/research/publications/ethical-guidelines-for-research-in-the-counselling-professions (accessed December 2020).

British Psychological Society (BPS) Code of Conduct, Ethical Principles and Guidelines – www.bps.org.uk/news-and-policy/bps-code-ethics-and-conduct (accessed December 2020).

British Sociological Association (BSA) Statement of Ethical Practice (2017) – www.britsoc.co.uk/ethics (accessed December 2020).

Dobson, C (2008) Conducting Research with People not Having the Capacity to Consent to their Participation: A Practical Guide for Researchers – www.ed.ac.uk/files/atoms/files/bps_guidelines_for_conducting_research_with_people_not_having_capacity_to_consent.pdf (accessed December 2020).

Economic and Social Research Council (ESRC) Ethical Framework – https://esrc.ukri.org/funding/guidance-for-applicants/research-ethics (accessed December 2020).

Economic and Social Research Council (ESRC) (2015) ESRC Framework for Research Ethics – https://esrc.ukri.org/files/funding/guidance-for-applicants/esrc-framework-for-research-ethics-2015 (accessed December 2020).

Express Scribe Transcription – http://help.nchsoftware.com/help/en/scribe/win/keys.html (accessed December 2020).

Flaherty C (2017) Past as Prologue – www.insidehighered.com/news/2017/04/25/controversy-over-alice-goffman-leads-pomona-students-say-her-alleged-racial (accessed December 2020).

General Data Protection Regulation (GDPR) https://gdpr-info.eu (accessed December 2020).

Health Research Authority (HRA) (2020a) HRA Approval – www.hra.nhs.uk/approvals-amendments/what-approvals-do-i-need/hra-approval (accessed December 2020).

Health Research Authority (HRA) (2020b) Mental Capacity Act – www.hra.nhs.uk/planning-and-improving-research/policies-standards-legislation/mental-capacity-act (accessed December 2020).

Integrated Research Application System (IRAS) www.myresearchproject.org.uk (accessed December 2020).

Mental Capacity Act (2005) Chapter 9 – www.legislation.gov.uk/ukpga/2005/9/pdfs/ukpga_20050009_en.pdf (accessed December 2020).

Office of the Public Guardian (2017) SD8: Safeguarding Policy, 4 July – www.gov.uk/government/publications/safeguarding-policy-protecting-vulnerable-adults/sd8-opgs-safeguarding-policy (accessed December 2020).

Social Research Association (SRA) Ethical Guidelines – https://the-sra.org.uk/SRA/Ethics/Ethics.aspx (accessed December 2020).

The Care Quality Commission (Gillick Competency) www.cqc.org.uk/guidance-providers/gps/nigels-surgery-8-gillick-competency-fraser-guidelines (accessed December 2020).

The Children Act (2004) www.legislation.gov.uk/ukpga/2004/31/contents (accessed December 2020).

UK Data Service – https://ukdataservice.ac.uk (accessed December 2020).

United Nations Convention on the Rights of the Child (UNCRC) (1989) www.unicef.org.uk/wp-content/uploads/2010/05/UNCRC_united_nations_convention_on_the_rights_of_the_child.pdf (accessed December 2020).

Wordbee Transcription Services – www.wordbee.co.uk (accessed December 2020).

INDEX

This index is in word-by-word alphabetical order. Figures and Tables are indicated by page numbers in bold print.